Women With ADHD

CRAFTED BY SKRIUWER

Copyright © 2024 by Skriuwer.

All rights reserved. No part of this book may be used or reproduced in any form whatsoever without written permission except in the case of brief quotations in critical articles or reviews.

For more information, contact : **kontakt@skriuwer.com** (www.skriuwer.com)

TABLE OF CONTENTS

CHAPTER 1: INTRODUCTION TO ADHD IN WOMEN

- How ADHD is misunderstood in girls and women
- Three core symptoms and their different expressions
- Why early diagnosis is often missed

CHAPTER 2: COMMON SIGNS AND SYMPTOMS

- Key indicators of inattention, hyperactivity, and impulsivity in adult women
- Emotional sensitivity and mood shifts
- How ADHD symptoms change over time

CHAPTER 3: SOCIETAL MYTHS AND MISUNDERSTANDINGS

- Misconceptions that ADHD only affects boys or is purely behavioral
- Stigma and how it delays women's diagnoses
- Challenging outdated beliefs and finding accurate information

CHAPTER 4: THE ROLE OF HORMONES

- How hormonal changes affect ADHD
- Shifts in symptoms at different life stages
- Tips for balancing hormones and ADHD treatment

CHAPTER 5: SCHOOL AND LEARNING

- ADHD's impact on studying, note-taking, and homework completion
- Practical classroom strategies and support services
- Self-advocacy and finding accommodations

CHAPTER 6: WORK AND CAREERS

- *ADHD hurdles in time management, deadlines, and workplace communication*
- *Choosing jobs that fit an ADHD-friendly environment*
- *Asking for accommodations and thriving professionally*

CHAPTER 7: ORGANIZATION AND TIME MANAGEMENT

- *Practical steps for decluttering, scheduling, and remembering tasks*
- *How to maintain a planner or app effectively*
- *Overcoming procrastination and distractions*

CHAPTER 8: PLANNING, GOALS, & FOLLOW-THROUGH

- *Breaking down large tasks into achievable steps*
- *Staying motivated when interest dips*
- *Tools to track progress and celebrate small wins*

CHAPTER 9: MANAGING STRESS AND ANXIETY

- *Why ADHD amplifies stress and worry*
- *Quick coping techniques for anxious moments*
- *Building long-term resilience and reducing overwhelm*

CHAPTER 10: RELATIONSHIPS AND COMMUNICATION

- *ADHD's influence on social cues, conversations, and conflict*
- *Improving listening skills and avoiding impulsive remarks*
- *Strengthening connections with friends, family, and partners*

CHAPTER 11: HEALTH AND SELF-CARE

- Establishing balanced routines for sleep, exercise, and nutrition
- Reducing burnout and creating realistic wellness habits
- Tools for stress relief and body confidence

CHAPTER 12: PARENTING WITH ADHD

- Challenges of juggling children's schedules alongside ADHD symptoms
- Setting family routines and delegating tasks
- Modeling healthy coping and communication for kids

CHAPTER 13: FRIENDSHIPS AND SOCIAL LIFE

- Handling forgetfulness, impulsivity, and social anxiety
- Finding hobbies or group activities to maintain friendships
- Balancing alone time with social connections

CHAPTER 14: SELF-CONFIDENCE AND SELF-ESTEEM

- Identifying negative thought patterns and self-talk
- Reframing mistakes as learning rather than failures
- Building a more balanced and positive self-image

CHAPTER 15: PERSONAL GROWTH AND EMOTIONAL WELL-BEING

- Exploring personal values and setting meaningful goals
- Mindful reflection for managing emotional swings
- Turning challenges into opportunities for growth

CHAPTER 16: MONEY MANAGEMENT

- Budgeting methods that fit ADHD tendencies
- Avoiding impulsive spending and late bill payments
- Saving strategies for long-term financial stability

CHAPTER 17: MINDFULNESS PRACTICES

- Short, easy techniques for a busy or restless mind
- Movement-based mindfulness (walking, stretching) for ADHD
- Reducing emotional reactivity through present-moment awareness

CHAPTER 18: HOBBIES AND PERSONAL INTERESTS

- Benefits of engaging hobbies for relaxation and creativity
- Choosing activities that match energy levels and interests
- Preventing boredom or overwhelm and balancing responsibilities

CHAPTER 19: WHEN TO SEEK PROFESSIONAL HELP

- Recognizing signs that self-guided methods are not enough
- What to expect from doctors, therapists, and ADHD coaches
- Overcoming fears about medication or therapy

CHAPTER 20: LOOKING AHEAD & FINDING HOPE

- Embracing long-term self-growth and adapting over life stages
- Maintaining supportive networks and positive routines
- Viewing ADHD as part of your story, not the defining factor

Chapter 1: Introduction to ADHD in Women

Attention Deficit Hyperactivity Disorder, known as ADHD, is a condition that affects how a person pays attention and manages impulses. Many people think of ADHD as something that only affects boys or men. This belief comes from the way ADHD was first studied and recognized. In earlier years, most of the research focused on hyperactive young boys. Teachers and parents noticed that certain boys had trouble staying in their seats or sticking to class rules, so these boys were diagnosed more often. However, this means that many girls and women went undiagnosed for a long time. When we understand that ADHD appears in women as well, it helps us see that the condition can look different in them. It also helps us realize that many women did not get the help they needed, sometimes even for many years.

ADHD has three main features: inattention, hyperactivity, and impulsivity. The condition can look different in every person. Some individuals are more inattentive, meaning they might daydream a lot or have trouble focusing. Others are more hyperactive, meaning they can be very energetic, move around a lot, and find it hard to stay still. Impulsivity means making quick decisions or actions without taking time to think about them first. A person might interrupt conversations, blurt out answers, or make hasty decisions. Each of these features can be present in girls and women, but not always in the same way they appear in boys and men.

In many girls, ADHD can be quiet and hard to see. Instead of running around in circles in the classroom, a girl with ADHD might stare out of the window and think about other things. She might doodle in her notebook or lose track of time. She could look like she is being shy or calm, even though her mind is full of ideas and thoughts. Because of this, teachers or parents might not suspect ADHD in girls. They might just think the girl is daydreaming or lazy. As a result, the girl might not get tested or diagnosed. She might go through her school years feeling that something is wrong with her, but never knowing what it is.

It is important to talk about how ADHD can affect women across different stages of life. A girl who was never diagnosed might go through high school doing her best to keep up. She might try extra hard to stay organized, or she might rely on friends and family members to remind her of assignments. Once she graduates and becomes an adult, there might be more responsibilities, such as college, a job, or taking care of a home. At that point, these responsibilities can become overwhelming. Managing time, remembering tasks, and staying organized can feel like a big challenge. A woman who has gone undiagnosed might not know why she struggles with these things. This can lead to stress and self-doubt. She may wonder why other people seem to handle everyday tasks with ease while she finds them hard to manage.

Another important point is that ADHD can influence emotions. Many women with ADHD might have strong feelings or react more than expected to certain situations. They might feel excitement, frustration, or sadness very deeply. This intensity of emotion can be linked to how their brains work. When these emotional reactions happen, a woman might feel embarrassed if people judge her for reacting in a big way. Over time, she might try to hide her real feelings, which can add more stress to her life.

We also need to understand that hormones play a role in a woman's life and can affect ADHD symptoms. For instance, changes in hormones during puberty, monthly cycles, pregnancy, and menopause can affect attention, mood, and energy. If a woman does not know she has ADHD, these hormonal changes can make her feel confused about why she is sometimes more forgetful or more moody than usual. She may blame herself and think she just needs to try harder or be more disciplined. This can lead to self-criticism and even depression or anxiety.

Sometimes, women with ADHD might develop ways to cope with their symptoms without knowing they have ADHD. They might keep lots of lists, spend more time on tasks that others finish quickly, or find a job where they can move around and avoid sitting in one place for too long. While these methods help, they can be tiring. A woman may feel exhausted from trying to keep up with everyone else. She might worry that people will think she is lazy or careless if they see her struggling with tasks that seem simple to others.

In the past, ADHD was mostly linked to young boys who misbehaved in class. Because of that, many women did not get diagnosed until adulthood. Some women only discovered they had ADHD after one of their children was diagnosed. When they learned about their child's ADHD symptoms, they recognized those same challenges in themselves. This is a big reason why understanding ADHD in women is so important. The sooner a woman recognizes the signs, the sooner she can get help and learn how to handle her symptoms. This can make a big difference in her relationships, career, and day-to-day life.

It is also important to know that ADHD is not a sign of laziness or lack of intelligence. ADHD is linked to how the brain works. Many women with ADHD are creative, capable, and bright. They often have a unique way of seeing the world and may have strengths in areas such as problem-solving or thinking outside the box. But because of challenges with attention, organization, or impulse control, they might have trouble meeting deadlines or keeping track of things. When a woman finally understands that she has ADHD, it can offer relief and help her find proper strategies. This new understanding can lower the blame and shame she might have felt for years.

Another issue women with ADHD face is that they might be more likely to deal with other mental health conditions. These can include anxiety and depression. Sometimes, these conditions arise because a woman has spent years feeling overwhelmed or criticized for forgetting things. She might have been told that she is irresponsible or careless. Over time, these negative messages can harm her self-esteem. A woman might think she cannot do things right or that she is not good enough. These thoughts can lead to anxiety or feelings of sadness. If she does not know that ADHD is the main issue, she might focus only on treating anxiety or depression. That approach might help a little, but it will not tackle the root cause of the struggles if ADHD goes undiagnosed.

Each person's ADHD is unique, but the need for knowledge is shared by many. By learning about how ADHD shows up in women, we can make sure fewer women remain undiagnosed or misunderstood. It is helpful for educators, doctors, and families to know the full picture of ADHD so they can spot signs early. It is also useful for women to learn that their struggles might have a name and that help is available.

In many parts of the world, there has been a growing interest in the experiences of women with ADHD. More online communities and support groups have formed. In these groups, women often share their personal challenges and talk about strategies that help them manage tasks and responsibilities. Hearing other people's stories can help a woman feel less alone. She might realize that she is not "broken." This knowledge can encourage her to explore ways to handle daily tasks in a way that suits her brain.

It is also important to note that ADHD does not look the same in all women. Some might be very chatty or social, while others might keep to themselves. Some women might be tidy in some areas but have piles of laundry they never touch. Others might have trouble remembering basic things, like where they put their keys or when they have an appointment. These different expressions of ADHD are all valid. It is a flexible condition that can take many forms. However, the common thread is that ADHD impacts attention, impulses, and sometimes hyperactivity.

Understanding ADHD in women can also involve looking at why it was overlooked in the past. Society often expects girls and women to be quiet, calm, and responsible. A girl who talks a lot or can't sit still might be labeled as "chatty" or "rude." She might be told to be more ladylike or polite. These labels do not hint at a medical condition like ADHD, so the behaviors are dismissed or misunderstood. In other cases, a girl might do well in school because she works really hard to meet everyone's expectations. But the effort it takes leaves her feeling drained and anxious. By the time she becomes an adult, this cycle of overworking to hide her symptoms can lead to burnout. Without the right help, she might feel stuck and hopeless.

Women with ADHD might also struggle in relationships. For example, forgetting birthdays or having trouble with routines can cause friction with a spouse or partner. Impulsive decisions might lead to money problems or arguments. ADHD can also affect communication if a woman forgets what was discussed or interrupts her partner in mid-sentence. Yet, these behaviors do not come from a desire to be rude or careless. They happen because the ADHD brain processes information differently. When the woman and her partner learn more about ADHD, they can create ways to handle these issues better. This can lower conflicts and help the couple be more patient with each other.

Some women might worry about getting help because they feel shame or fear that others will think less of them. It can be hard to visit a doctor or mental health professional and talk about personal struggles. However, seeking help can make a big difference. Getting a proper evaluation is the first step toward understanding why certain problems keep happening. A doctor or therapist can suggest treatment options such as counseling, medication, or organizational strategies. Learning about ADHD and how it affects a person can bring a sense of relief. A woman might realize that she is not alone and that there are many others facing similar problems.

In addition to official treatment, it can help a lot to talk to friends or family members who are supportive. A caring friend or relative might help by reminding a woman about appointments or offering encouragement. At times, just having someone who listens and understands can make things feel less overwhelming. It is also helpful to write down tasks or plans. Even something as simple as putting sticky notes around the house or keeping a planner on the kitchen table can ease stress.

As we move forward in this book, we will talk about the many areas of life where ADHD can have an impact. We will look at practical ideas for managing school, work, and relationships. We will also talk about the emotions that come with ADHD and how to handle stress and self-doubt. The first step is always learning more about ADHD, so women can begin to see themselves in a more understanding way. Once you know how ADHD works, you can look for ways to adjust your life to match your own style of thinking and doing things.

For now, the important idea to hold on to is that ADHD in women is real and common. It might look different than in men, which is why it has been overlooked so often. A woman with ADHD might feel like she has to do twice as much work just to keep up with daily tasks. If she does not understand why, she might be harsh on herself or think she is not smart enough. But ADHD does not mean a person lacks intelligence or ability. It simply means the brain functions in a unique way. Recognizing ADHD is a step toward finding methods to handle it and lower the stress it causes.

All of this brings us to a clear understanding: when ADHD is recognized, women can find better ways to handle their responsibilities and emotions. They can learn techniques that match how their brains work. They can also stop blaming themselves for problems that are not their fault. With knowledge comes the power to make small changes that bring about positive results. This book is written to share information, tips, and hope. Each person's situation is different, but the aim is to offer a foundation that can be adapted. If you suspect you have ADHD or have already been diagnosed, you are not alone. Many other women are in the same place. By continuing to learn and find ideas that suit your specific needs, you can make progress in your life in a way that feels right for you.

Chapter 2: Common Signs and Symptoms

Women with ADHD often notice certain patterns in their daily habits, emotions, and reactions. These patterns can be seen as signs and symptoms that point to differences in how the brain processes information. In the past, people believed that the main signs of ADHD were hyperactivity and impulsiveness. However, in women, inattentiveness often stands out more. This inattentiveness can show up in ways that might be mistaken for laziness or forgetfulness. That is why it is helpful to understand the different ways ADHD can reveal itself.

Below, we will look at some of the more common signs and symptoms found in women. Not every woman will experience all of these signs, but noticing several of them might suggest that ADHD could be present. If a woman recognizes these behaviors in herself or a loved one, it might be time to seek an evaluation. An official evaluation from a qualified professional is the best way to confirm whether ADHD is indeed part of the picture.

---

1. Inattentiveness and Distractibility

A common sign of ADHD in women is the struggle with keeping focused on tasks, conversations, or other important details. A woman might find that her mind tends to wander, especially when a task is uninteresting or repetitive. In a classroom setting, a teacher might notice that a girl stares out of the window or looks lost in thought. At work, a woman might have a tough time sitting through long meetings. She might find it difficult to focus on paperwork or detailed tasks without feeling restless.

This loss of focus can cause mistakes, such as forgetting to follow important steps in a task. For example, a woman might leave out a main ingredient in a recipe, even though she has made that dish many times before. When speaking with friends or coworkers, she might lose track of what is being said. She might need to ask, "Can you repeat that?" because her mind drifted elsewhere. These moments of inattention can be frustrating, especially if others view them as a lack of concern.

Distractibility can also appear in a woman's environment. She might start working on a project at home, but then remember she needs to do the laundry. While heading to the laundry room, she might see a book on the table and start reading it. After that, she might notice her phone buzzing and pick it up to check messages. Eventually, she forgets about the laundry entirely. This chain of distractions is common in women with ADHD. Tasks can remain half-finished, leading to clutter or confusion around the house.

---

2. Hyperactivity and Restlessness

Although many women with ADHD lean toward inattentiveness, hyperactivity can still appear in some women. However, it might look different than what we usually see in young boys who cannot sit still. A woman with ADHD might tap her foot, drum her fingers, or fidget with objects like pens or paper. She might feel uneasy when required to stay seated for a long time. She might also be drawn to activities that allow her to move around, such as going for a walk or stretching, to release extra energy.

This restlessness can appear in her thoughts as well. Her mind might move quickly from one idea to another. Sometimes, this can lead to creative thinking, but it can also feel like a constant rush of thoughts that never settles down. At night, she might have difficulty winding down to sleep because her mind is still busy. This can lead to tiredness during the day, creating a cycle of exhaustion and a need to stay in motion.

Hyperactivity does not always mean a person is physically bouncing around. It can also be mental or emotional agitation. For example, a woman might start many new projects at once, only to drop them partway through. She might feel like she always needs to be doing something or else she feels uneasy. This can cause stress or burnout if it goes on for too long without rest or relaxation.

---

3. Impulsivity in Speech and Actions

Impulsivity means acting quickly without thinking through the potential results. For women with ADHD, impulsivity might come across in different ways. One example is interrupting people during a conversation. She may not mean to be rude, but she has a thought and feels the urge to share it right away. Another example is making quick decisions about purchases. She might buy items online without fully considering whether she can afford them or truly needs them.

Impulsivity can also show up in relationships. A woman with ADHD might send a text message or email in the heat of the moment. Later, she might regret sending it, realizing that she acted on temporary emotions. In some cases, impulsivity can lead to risk-taking behaviors, such as impulsive driving or risky financial choices. Of course, not all women with ADHD take big risks, but the tendency to act first and think later can still affect day-to-day life.

This habit of acting on impulses can create problems over time. Friends or coworkers might feel that the woman does not respect their boundaries because she cuts in or interrupts. In romantic relationships, the woman might say things she does not really mean during an argument. She could also make major life changes on a whim, such as quitting a job without planning for what comes next. Recognizing impulsivity is the first step to managing it in a healthier way.

---

4. Strong Emotions and Mood Shifts

Women with ADHD often feel their emotions in a powerful way. A simple setback can cause a wave of frustration or sadness. A minor success can spark big excitement. These emotional ups and downs can be confusing if a woman does not realize that her mind processes feelings with greater intensity than others. She might think there is something wrong with her for feeling things so strongly.

These sharp emotional shifts can affect relationships at home, at work, or with friends. For instance, a sudden burst of anger over something small might surprise people who do not know about her ADHD. Later, the woman might feel guilty or embarrassed for losing her temper. Over time, these repeated emotional swings can lead to tension or misunderstandings. She might also avoid talking about her feelings because she worries about being judged for how she reacts.

A related issue is "rejection sensitivity," which some women with ADHD experience. This means feeling anxious or extremely upset over the possibility of being rejected or criticized by others. The fear of letting people down can create a lot of stress. The woman might say yes to tasks she cannot handle because she is afraid of disappointing others. She might read negative meaning into an innocent remark from a friend. Understanding that her brain processes feelings differently can help her step back and consider the situation more calmly.

5. Disorganization and Forgetfulness

For many women with ADHD, day-to-day organization can be a major problem. Keeping track of appointments, bills, and household responsibilities can feel overwhelming. Items might pile up in random spots. Important documents might be lost or misplaced. In school, this disorganization could lead a girl to lose homework or forget about tests. As an adult, a woman might miss deadlines at work or accidentally pay bills late.

Forgetting things is common. She might forget birthdays or scheduled events even if she wrote them down. She might walk into a room and forget why she went there in the first place. She could lock herself out of the house because she left her keys on the counter. These small lapses might happen frequently, causing her to feel embarrassed or unreliable. Other people might criticize her for not being responsible, which can wear on her self-esteem.

Sometimes, a woman with ADHD will attempt to be more organized by setting up planners or to-do lists. But if she is inconsistent in using these tools, the problem remains. She might buy a nice planner and then forget to open it for days. She could create color-coded folders for her papers, but then leave them scattered around the house. The main issue is not that she does not want to be organized, but that her brain struggles to maintain the routines that keep life in order.

---

6. Trouble with Time Management

Time management is another big challenge for many women with ADHD. They might lose track of time while focusing on a task they find interesting, or they might procrastinate on tasks they find dull or scary. They could be late for meetings, events, or social appointments without meaning to be. The passage of time can feel uneven for them. A simple job might stretch on longer than expected, making them scramble at the last minute to get everything else done.

Some women with ADHD find themselves cramming tasks into the last possible moment. This rush can lead to mistakes or added stress. They might vow never to do it again, but the pattern repeats if they do not address the underlying reason. Others might hop from one task to another without finishing anything, because they are drawn to whatever seems interesting at the time. This can create chaos in their day, making it hard to see real progress.

Time management struggles can make it difficult to keep a steady routine. If a woman is supposed to wake up early, she might sleep through her alarm because she stayed up too late the night before. If she plans to cook dinner at a certain time, she might get distracted by a TV show or a phone call. By the time she remembers, it could be much later than planned. These setbacks may seem small when viewed one by one, but they can add up and disrupt her entire schedule.

---

7. Challenges with Following Through

For women with ADHD, starting a new task can feel exciting, especially if it is something they are interested in. They might gather supplies, talk about their ideas with others, and put a lot of effort into the initial phase. But once the novelty wears off, it becomes harder to keep going. They might lose interest or become distracted by another idea. As a result, they could have several unfinished crafts, half-written stories, or incomplete personal projects around the house.

Following through can also be a problem for responsibilities that involve many steps, such as planning a large family event or finishing a series of tasks at work. Each step might seem manageable on its own, but putting them all together can be too much. A woman with ADHD might feel uncertain about where to start or which tasks to do in what order. She might freeze or look for other things to do, allowing the main task to remain unfinished.

This difficulty with follow-through can affect how others see her. They might think she is lazy or untrustworthy. They may be hesitant to ask for her help if they believe she will not complete the job. This can be discouraging for the woman, who might feel eager to help but cannot keep up the effort needed to finish. Feeling like she is letting people down can take a toll on her self-esteem.

---

8. Possible Co-Existing Problems

Women with ADHD often face other mental health or emotional problems alongside their ADHD symptoms. Two of the most common are anxiety and depression. Anxiety can arise from years of feeling disorganized, forgetting tasks, and worrying about what others think. A woman might lie awake at night, replaying mistakes or dreading the next day's tasks. Depression can emerge if she feels stuck, isolated, or ashamed about her struggles.

Eating problems might also occur. Some women with ADHD have disordered eating patterns because they forget to eat at regular times or they eat impulsively. Others might use food to handle stress or boredom. Sleep issues are another possibility. Trouble settling down at night can make it hard to get the rest needed to function well the next day. If these extra problems are not addressed, they can add to the stress of living with ADHD.

Substance abuse can sometimes appear in women with ADHD. This can be related to impulsivity or an attempt to manage emotional pain. Not all women with ADHD deal with substance abuse, but it is important to be aware that it can happen. If a woman is feeling overwhelmed or unable to cope with her symptoms, she might look for escapes in unhealthy ways. Recognizing ADHD early and getting help can lower the risk of turning to harmful coping methods.

---

9. Signs That Appear at Different Life Stages

ADHD can show up in various ways depending on a woman's age and life situation. During childhood, a girl might daydream a lot, talk excessively, or get lost in creative worlds. She might be labeled a "chatterbox" or "spacy." Teen years can bring new challenges, as middle school and high school require more organization, time management, and social skills. A teen girl might struggle to balance homework with social activities. She might feel anxious about remembering details and meeting deadlines. Friendships might be hard to maintain if she blurts out things without thinking.

When a woman goes to college or starts a job, the need to manage many tasks on her own increases. She might have difficulty planning her schedule, keeping up with bills, or handling the responsibilities of daily living. If she also decides to have children, the chaos can multiply. She might feel overwhelmed by taking care of a child's needs while also juggling household tasks. Hormonal changes during pregnancy can also affect ADHD symptoms, sometimes making them worse or, in some cases, temporarily easing them.

Later in life, menopause can bring its own hormone changes, which may affect memory and attention. A woman with ADHD might feel her symptoms become more obvious, or that she is less able to compensate for them. The demands of caring for older parents or dealing with job changes can also create more stress. In each life stage, ADHD might show up differently, but the root cause remains the same. Being aware of how symptoms can shift helps a woman plan ways to manage them.

---

10. Why These Signs and Symptoms Are Often Missed

ADHD in women is overlooked for several reasons. One reason is that many people imagine a hyperactive boy running around a classroom when they think of ADHD. A quiet daydreaming girl does not fit that image. Therefore, she might not get a second look from teachers or doctors. Another reason is that girls and women are often taught to hide their problems and be people-pleasers. They may try to keep up with tasks by forcing themselves to pay extra attention or by asking for help in ways that do not draw too much notice. As a result, their struggles might be hidden until adulthood, when life demands become too big to handle on their own.

Additionally, many healthcare professionals in the past were not trained to see the specific ways ADHD appears in women. This can lead to women being labeled with anxiety or depression without looking for the root cause. While anxiety and depression can be part of the picture, ADHD may be the main issue. When ADHD is not recognized, the treatment might not work as well as it could. The woman might then blame herself, thinking she is not trying hard enough to feel better.

Cultural expectations also play a role. In some communities, women are expected to be extra responsible for their families, homes, and social connections. A woman with ADHD who struggles to plan meals, remember events, or manage children's schedules might be seen as a failure by society's standards. Instead of looking for a medical reason behind her difficulties, others might think she is just not making enough effort. These judgments can cause shame, making the woman less likely to seek help or talk about her issues.

11. Recognizing the Need for Support

Understanding these common signs and symptoms can help a woman decide if she should speak with a professional. If a woman sees these patterns in herself and they cause real problems in her daily life, it is worth seeking an evaluation. A proper diagnosis can open the door to help and support. Knowing there is a reason behind her struggles can be a relief. It can also guide her toward specific methods for handling tasks, emotions, and relationships.

For example, if a woman often forgets appointments, she might use electronic reminders or alarms on her phone. If she struggles with impulsive spending, she can plan her budget more carefully or ask a trusted friend to help her stay accountable. If emotional ups and downs are the main issue, she could learn calming techniques or find a counselor. Each sign or symptom can be managed in different ways. The key is to recognize them first, so the right support can be found.

Some women feel uncertain about labeling themselves with ADHD, worried about the stigma attached. But having a label does not define a person's worth. Instead, it can be a way to describe how the brain functions. By naming it, a woman can locate resources, learn new skills, and talk openly with family members or friends about what she needs. It can also help her realize that she is not alone and that many others face similar challenges.

---

12. Moving Forward

By seeing these signs and symptoms for what they are, women can begin to look at their patterns and habits more clearly. They can question whether their attention, organization, and emotional control problems might be due to ADHD. Once they suspect ADHD, the next step is to talk to a professional. A trained doctor, therapist, or psychiatrist can perform an evaluation and recommend treatments. These treatments might include counseling, medication, or lifestyle adjustments.

Self-awareness is an important part of this process. A woman might realize that she is not flawed or lazy. Instead, she has a brain that works differently. With that knowledge, she can be kinder to herself and be open to learning new methods. It might involve trial and error to find what works best for her. But each change she makes can bring her closer to a daily routine that feels more manageable. She might also reach out to other women with ADHD, either online or in person, for advice and understanding.

It is helpful to keep in mind that ADHD is not all negative. Many women with ADHD show great creativity, originality, or high energy. They might be excellent at coming up with ideas or finding new solutions to problems. They can be fun and lively in social settings. The goal is to build on these positive traits while managing the challenging ones. Understanding these symptoms is the starting point for making life more balanced and stable.

This completes our look at the common signs and symptoms of ADHD in women. Each person is different, so not everything listed will apply to every woman. However, being aware of these key patterns makes it easier to see if ADHD could be a factor. In the upcoming chapters, we will explore more specific areas of life such as work, relationships, self-care, and more. The hope is that women will see how ADHD might affect them in all kinds of ways and learn approaches that fit their needs. By doing so, they can reduce stress, improve self-esteem, and create structures in their lives that help them thrive.

Chapter 3: Societal Myths and Misunderstandings

ADHD in women has long been overlooked or misunderstood by society. Many people cling to certain myths about ADHD that make it harder for women to receive the proper help. These myths can come from old research, media portrayals, or even from friends and family who do not realize how ADHD truly works. Understanding these myths helps us see why women often go undiagnosed or feel unsupported.

Below, we will discuss some of the most widespread myths and misunderstandings. We will look at how these myths developed, why they continue, and what we can do to counter them. By breaking down these false ideas, women with ADHD can feel less guilt and more acceptance of what they face.

---

1. **Myth: ADHD Only Affects Children, Especially Boys**

One of the biggest myths is that ADHD is something that only shows up in childhood. Many people believe that if a person was not diagnosed as a child, then they cannot have ADHD. This view comes from the fact that ADHD was historically studied in young boys who behaved in hyperactive ways in school. Early research often looked at boys who fidgeted, spoke out of turn, and had trouble staying seated in the classroom.

Because of this limited focus, people did not pay much attention to how ADHD might look in girls. Girls were often quieter and may have shown inattentive symptoms, such as daydreaming. These behaviors were not considered as disruptive. As a result, many girls were missed in the diagnostic process, and they carried their undiagnosed ADHD into adulthood. This led to the false idea that ADHD mainly affects young boys. In truth, ADHD can appear in people of all ages and genders. It simply appears in different ways depending on the person.

Some adults believe they "grew out" of ADHD, so they assume that if a woman reaches adulthood without a diagnosis, she must not have it. In reality, some symptoms can shift as a person ages, but that does not mean the ADHD goes away. A girl who was able to pass through school by working extra hard might reach adulthood and find that the demands of daily life increase her challenges. As soon as she has to manage time, finances, family tasks, and work responsibilities, her ADHD might become more obvious.

---

2. **Myth: ADHD Is Not Real**

Another myth is that ADHD is not a valid condition, and that people who claim to have ADHD are just lazy or unfocused. Some hold the view that ADHD is an excuse to avoid responsibility. They might say, "Everyone gets distracted sometimes," or, "We all have trouble sitting still." While it is true that everyone can be distracted once in a while, ADHD involves a set of symptoms that are more frequent and serious than what most people experience. These symptoms can disrupt work, home life, and personal relationships.

There is strong scientific evidence that ADHD is linked to how the brain processes information, controls impulses, and regulates attention. Researchers have found differences in brain activity for people with ADHD compared to those without it. While some may remain skeptical, leading medical associations recognize ADHD as a real and treatable condition. Suggesting that it is "not real" can prevent women from getting the support they need. It also adds to the shame some women may feel about their struggles.

This myth can come from a misunderstanding of ADHD's more subtle signs. People might imagine only a hyperactive boy yelling in class. They do not see the quiet woman who forgets to pay her bills on time or struggles to focus on a work project. Because her struggles are less visible, others might doubt she has a real condition. This doubt can cause her to question her own experiences, making her delay seeking professional help.

---

3. Myth: ADHD Is Only Hyperactivity

When people think of ADHD, they often picture someone who is bouncing off the walls, running around, or speaking out of turn. This can lead to the belief that if a person is not hyperactive, they cannot have ADHD. Women with ADHD, though, are more likely to show inattentive symptoms, such as losing track of conversations or misplacing items around the house. They may also have internal restlessness, which is not as obvious to outside observers.

Some women do experience hyperactivity, but it might appear in a different way than in boys. Rather than climbing on furniture, a woman might tap her feet, shift in her seat, or fidget constantly. She might feel a strong need to move or stay busy, even though she looks calm on the outside. If people do not recognize this as a sign of ADHD, they might ignore her signs altogether. This can cause the woman to blame herself or assume that she simply lacks willpower.

Another aspect is mental hyperactivity. A woman's thoughts may race, jumping from one idea to the next. Even if her body is still, her mind can be active, making it tough to focus on a single task. Because this sort of hyperactivity is hidden, it can go unnoticed by observers and lead to the assumption that she is fine or just scattered.

4. **Myth: It Is a "Boy's Condition," So Girls Are Less Likely to Have It**

Closely linked to the first myth, this misunderstanding claims that ADHD is much rarer in girls. The truth is that boys are indeed diagnosed with ADHD more often in childhood. However, experts agree that many girls likely go undiagnosed because their signs look different. They might be more inattentive than hyperactive, and teachers or parents might see them as daydreamers or "quiet kids." Since they do not cause disruptions in class, adults overlook their challenges.

As these girls become women, they might develop strategies to hide their struggles. For example, they may spend hours each evening preparing for the next day, making elaborate to-do lists, or reviewing notes many times just to keep up. They might avoid social events so they can stay home and catch up on tasks they cannot finish quickly. Because they appear responsible and quiet, friends and family may not realize how much effort is required for them to function in a typical routine.

This myth can also make women doubt themselves. They might think, "ADHD is for boys who act out. I'm just unorganized." Such beliefs cause women to ignore their symptoms or blame their personality. This can delay a formal diagnosis and keep them from finding real solutions that could help. It is important to recognize that both men and women can have ADHD, even if it is expressed in different ways.

5. **Myth: ADHD Always Comes with Bad Behavior**

Some people assume that those with ADHD are troublemakers who cannot follow rules. They view ADHD as tied to misbehaving or acting out. This does happen in some cases, especially if the person is hyperactive or impulsive, but not everyone with ADHD shows disruptive behavior. Many women with ADHD have never been in trouble at school or work. They might even be people who follow the rules carefully because they fear getting into trouble. Despite that, they still deal with attention problems, disorganization, or forgetfulness.

This myth can be extra harmful because it implies a moral flaw. It makes it seem like if a woman is not misbehaving, then she must not really have ADHD. In reality, ADHD is about how the brain handles attention and impulses. A woman might follow directions exactly, but internally, she may be fighting to stay focused or to keep her emotions under control. She might also have outbursts at home, where she feels safe to show her stress, even though she appears well-behaved in public.

Another angle is that some women with ADHD might have acted out in their teen years but changed their behavior as adults. They could have learned to adapt or hide their impulsivity. People who knew them as teens might remember their rebellious phase and assume they simply grew out of it, not realizing that ADHD can still be present in many forms.

---

6. **Myth: You Can "Try Harder" and Fix ADHD**

There is a common misconception that ADHD is just a lack of effort or discipline. Some people might tell a woman, "Just be more organized," or, "You need to make yourself pay attention." While small changes in routine can help, ADHD is not solved just by willpower. It involves differences in how the brain functions, and these differences do not vanish through pure determination.

This idea can push women to blame themselves. They think, "If I just worked harder, I would not forget appointments." In turn, they might hide their struggles, feeling embarrassed for not measuring up. However, willpower alone will not fix the underlying issue. True management of ADHD often involves a combination of strategies, like cognitive-behavioral therapy, medication, supportive routines, and understanding from those around them.

It is helpful to remember that effort does matter, but it must be directed in a way that matches how the brain works. Telling someone with ADHD to simply "try harder" is like telling a person with poor eyesight to "see better" without offering them glasses. Support, tools, and accommodations can help a person with ADHD make full use of their abilities.

---

7. **Myth: ADHD Always Looks the Same in Everyone**

People often picture a single type of ADHD. They might imagine a child running around or a teen who is always late. However, ADHD can show up differently from one individual to another. Some women might primarily have inattentive symptoms, like losing things, drifting off, or struggling to complete tasks. Others might have more impulsive or hyperactive tendencies. And there are those who have a combined type.

Even among women who share the same general symptom type, ADHD can vary based on personality, upbringing, culture, and environment. For example, one woman might be very outgoing and talkative, while another might be quiet and introverted. Both can have ADHD, but their behaviors will not look the same. Assuming that ADHD has only one pattern can lead people to miss the signs in women who do not fit the common picture.

Accepting that ADHD can appear in many ways can help people be more open to noticing signs in themselves or others. It also lowers the risk of making quick judgments. A woman who is orderly in certain areas could still have ADHD if she struggles with other tasks. Another woman might be easygoing but has huge problems managing her finances. These are different expressions of the same underlying condition.

---

8. Myth: Media Portrayals Are Always Accurate

News stories, TV shows, and movies sometimes show characters with ADHD. While this can raise awareness, these portrayals can also spread false ideas. For example, a show might feature a restless teen who cannot stop talking, but never show a quiet young woman who fails to finish assignments on time. If viewers only see one type of ADHD character, they may assume that is the only valid expression.

Some media stories also focus too much on medication debates, painting ADHD as either a made-up condition or something solved solely by medication. These extremes ignore the fact that ADHD is complex. Treatment often involves multiple approaches, including therapy, life strategies, and sometimes medication. It is important to be aware that media outlets might oversimplify the topic to grab attention, missing the wider context of how ADHD affects people in real life.

Women with ADHD might compare themselves to a character in a show and decide they cannot have ADHD because they are not exactly the same. Or they may think their ADHD should fit a neat, dramatic storyline. In reality, life is more varied. Media can spark conversations, but real education about ADHD comes from credible sources such as medical experts, scientific research, and personal accounts from those living with the condition.

9. **Myth: Women with ADHD Are Always Disorganized and Messy**

Another myth is that all women with ADHD are completely disorganized or messy. Although many do have trouble with organization, this is not universal. Some women manage their ADHD by developing rigid systems or routines, so they can appear very tidy. They might keep color-coded schedules or follow strict habits to avoid losing track of details. Others might be organized at work but messy at home, or the opposite. The condition does not mean a person must be disorganized in every area of life.

In fact, some women manage to keep up a neat exterior because they spend much of their free time trying to stay in control. They could spend hours cleaning or arranging things, driven by a fear of being labeled lazy. This can be exhausting. On the other hand, some women accept a certain level of mess and focus their efforts on other tasks. Each person's relationship with organization is different.

Believing that all women with ADHD must be messy can lead to missed diagnoses if a woman is actually very neat. She may not see how her memory lapses, time management troubles, or emotional ups and downs could still point to ADHD. It is helpful to move past this stereotype and realize that there is no one-size-fits-all approach to ADHD.

10. **Myth: Women with ADHD Are Less Capable**

A harmful misunderstanding is that people with ADHD are less capable in school, work, or other tasks. Women with ADHD might internalize this belief and feel that they will never succeed. In fact, many women with ADHD are highly intelligent, creative, and resourceful. They often develop unique ways of handling problems. Some excel in fields that benefit from their fast thinking or big-picture view.

While ADHD can cause hurdles with planning, memory, or focus, it does not take away a person's potential. With the right support and understanding, many women with ADHD reach high levels of success. They might become well-respected leaders or innovators. The key is figuring out strategies that fit their style of thinking, rather than trying to force themselves into a mold that does not work for them.

Still, the myth of being less capable can linger, especially if a woman has faced criticisms for being scattered or forgetful. She might downplay her strengths or avoid taking on new challenges. This is why it is crucial to recognize and challenge this myth. Women with ADHD can perform at a high level when they have a fair environment that acknowledges their strengths and respects their struggles.

---

11. **Myth: If a Woman Was Successful in School or Work, She Can't Have ADHD**

Some people assume that ADHD always leads to poor performance in school or work. While ADHD can make these areas more challenging, not everyone with ADHD struggles academically. Many women do well because they develop coping methods. They might study longer, review notes repeatedly, or rely on technology and reminders to keep track of assignments. If their efforts pay off, they might get good grades or succeed in their job.

However, this success can hide the actual difficulty behind the scenes. A woman might be using more energy than her peers to keep up with daily tasks. She might feel constant stress because she fears that if she drops any of her coping routines, everything will fall apart. If teachers or bosses only see the end results, they may have no idea how much pressure she is under.

Later in life, when responsibilities grow (like managing a household, children, or more complex job duties), the coping methods may no longer work. She might suddenly find herself falling behind, not knowing that ADHD is at the core of it. It is important to realize that being successful in some areas does not rule out ADHD. Instead, it often means the person has worked very hard to handle challenges in ways that are not obvious.

---

12. Why Do These Myths Continue?

There are many reasons these myths remain. One reason is that older research focused on boys. Medical textbooks and training programs passed along this limited perspective. Over time, these ideas took root in public opinion. Another reason is that ADHD can be hard to see in women, especially those who hide their symptoms behind people-pleasing or perfectionism. Friends, family, and even some professionals might not realize what is happening unless they have up-to-date knowledge about ADHD.

Social standards also play a part. Girls and women are often expected to manage their emotions, be organized, and handle many responsibilities at once. When they struggle, people might judge them harshly. Rather than suspecting ADHD, observers might think the woman is not trying. This keeps the false ideas alive. Media portrayals can also feed these myths by focusing on flashy, dramatic forms of ADHD. Quiet or hidden ADHD stories rarely make the headlines.

---

13. Consequences of Myths and Misunderstandings

When myths go unchallenged, they can lead to missed diagnoses. Women may suffer through life without knowing they have ADHD. They might blame themselves for struggles they cannot control, leading to shame, anxiety, or depression. Even if they do seek help, they might face dismissive comments from people who believe the myths. This can discourage them from pursuing further evaluation or treatment.

These misunderstandings also affect professional relationships. A woman might be passed over for a promotion because her boss thinks she is careless, not realizing that ADHD is at play. In families, myths can create tension if relatives believe the woman is just being lazy or irresponsible. These conflicts add to the stress she already feels. Finally, myths can shape policy and educational practices, leading to a lack of resources for women and girls with ADHD.

---

14. Pushing Back Against Myths

The first step in rejecting these myths is spreading accurate information. People need to learn how ADHD appears in women and why it can be overlooked. Women who suspect they have ADHD can find specialists who understand adult ADHD and the different ways it shows up. Speaking openly about ADHD experiences can help dismantle false ideas. When friends or relatives see a real example of

ADHD in a person they know, they may begin to question their old beliefs.

It is also helpful to seek resources from medical associations, scientific studies, or trusted professionals. By pointing to reputable sources, women can show that ADHD is backed by evidence. They can also join or form support groups with others who have ADHD. This can build a sense of community and allow for the sharing of tips on handling tasks and responsibilities.

Teachers, counselors, and employers can play a part by educating themselves about ADHD in women. If they know the signs, they can be more understanding and supportive. When a teacher sees a girl who is quiet but seems disengaged, they can take steps to see if ADHD is a factor. When an employer sees an otherwise skilled worker who struggles with deadlines, they can explore ways to support her, such as allowing flexible schedules or using digital reminders.

---

15. Moving Forward with Knowledge

Understanding that ADHD is not just a "boy's condition" or the result of laziness opens the door for more realistic support. Myths and misunderstandings hurt women by leaving them feeling judged and alone. Once the false ideas are challenged, women can feel free to seek the help they need. They might pursue an official evaluation, try new tools for organizing, or explore treatments that make sense for their situation.

As more people learn about women's experiences with ADHD, the stigma lessens. Society can move toward a more accurate view of ADHD as a condition that affects people in different ways. This shift in perspective benefits not only those with ADHD but also their families, workplaces, and communities. When we replace myths with understanding, we create an environment where women feel confident reaching out for guidance and growth in the face of ADHD.

That is the goal: to ensure that false beliefs do not hold women back from recognizing and managing their ADHD. Through awareness, education, and compassion, society can dispel these myths and give women a fair chance to succeed. The chapters ahead will offer more information about handling various parts of life with ADHD, from hormone changes to relationships. Armed with correct facts, women can make informed choices and find paths that work best for their own minds.

Chapter 4: The Role of Hormones

Hormones play a large part in how the body and brain function. For women with ADHD, hormone fluctuations can make symptoms change or become more intense at certain points in life. Understanding the link between hormones and ADHD can help women plan ahead. It also shows why ADHD might become more noticeable at certain life stages, such as during puberty, pregnancy, or menopause.

In this chapter, we will look at how hormonal changes influence the brain and body, and why these shifts can affect attention, impulsivity, and mood. Recognizing these connections can lead to better management methods for women with ADHD.

---

1. **Basic Overview of Hormones**

Hormones are chemical messengers that move throughout the body. They affect growth, mood, energy levels, and many other functions. In women, the main sex hormones are estrogen and progesterone. These shift throughout the monthly cycle, as well as during puberty, pregnancy, and menopause. Other hormones, such as cortisol (related to stress) and thyroid hormones, can also have an impact on how a person feels day to day.

The brain is sensitive to changes in hormone levels. Some parts of the brain help regulate attention and impulse control. These parts include the prefrontal cortex, which is involved in planning and decision-making. Hormones can alter how the brain cells in these regions function. For women with ADHD, any sudden or large change in hormone levels might affect their ability to focus, stay calm, or control their impulses.

2. Puberty and the Start of Hormone Changes

Puberty is one of the first major hormonal shifts in a girl's life. During this time, estrogen and progesterone levels rise, leading to physical changes. Puberty can also bring emotional changes, as the mind adjusts to these new hormone levels. For a girl with ADHD, puberty can be a time when symptoms become more visible. She might have managed her attention issues fairly well as a child, or her signs might have been mild enough to go unnoticed. But as her hormones start fluctuating, her mood and focus can vary more than before.

In some cases, puberty can make her inattentive symptoms seem worse, because she might have more responsibilities in school and at home while also dealing with the stress of physical changes. She could have less patience for things that bore her. She might find that her emotions are stronger, leading to tearfulness or anger over small issues. If she does not realize that ADHD is part of the reason, she might blame her teenage hormones alone. But understanding that ADHD can become more obvious during puberty helps parents, teachers, and healthcare providers offer the right support.

---

3. Monthly Hormone Cycles

Once a girl reaches puberty, her body goes through a monthly cycle. Estrogen rises and falls, as does progesterone. Some women with ADHD notice that their ability to focus or manage tasks changes at different times of the month. For instance, they might feel more energetic and clear-headed when estrogen is higher, and more forgetful or irritable when it drops. These shifts can lead to a cycle of good days and bad days, making it tough to maintain a steady routine.

This pattern can also cause confusion if a woman does not track her cycle. She might feel fine and productive for a couple of weeks, only to become anxious or scattered later. If she is unaware of the connection to hormones, she may feel like she is unpredictable or moody for no clear reason. Some doctors and therapists suggest that women with ADHD keep a journal of their mood and focus levels throughout the month. This can help them see if there is a link to hormone changes.

Some women with ADHD also report worse premenstrual symptoms, such as strong mood swings, cravings, or fatigue. This can be partly due to the drop in estrogen before the period starts. If a woman's ADHD includes a tendency toward strong emotions, premenstrual shifts may feel especially intense. While not all women with ADHD experience severe premenstrual problems, enough do that it is worth acknowledging.

---

4. **Pregnancy and Postpartum**

Another key time of hormonal change is pregnancy. During pregnancy, estrogen and progesterone rise to help sustain the pregnancy and support fetal development. For some women with ADHD, these higher levels of estrogen can lessen their symptoms for a while, improving their mood or focus. Others may not notice much difference. Each body is unique, and hormone sensitivity can differ from one woman to another.

However, after giving birth, hormone levels drop quickly, which can cause fatigue and emotional changes known as "baby blues." For some new mothers with ADHD, the postpartum period can be especially difficult. They might feel overwhelmed by the demands of caring for a newborn while dealing with fluctuating hormones. Lack of sleep can also worsen ADHD symptoms, as being tired makes it harder to stay organized or calm.

Postpartum depression can be a real risk, particularly if a woman has struggled with mood issues before. ADHD can make these feelings stronger, as the woman might judge herself harshly for not handling tasks well. She might also worry about forgetting important tasks related to the baby's care. Seeking help from a healthcare professional, a counselor, or a support group can make a big difference during this stage.

---

5. **Birth Control and Hormonal Treatments**

Some women with ADHD choose to use birth control methods that involve hormones, such as the pill, patch, or ring. These can affect the balance of estrogen and progesterone in the body. Some women find that certain types of birth control help stabilize mood and reduce shifts in attention. Others might find that hormonal birth control makes their ADHD-related emotional swings worse. Since each body reacts differently to these treatments, it is important to monitor changes when starting or switching birth control methods.

If a woman notices that her ADHD symptoms get worse after starting a new hormonal contraceptive, she might want to talk to her doctor about trying a different option. It can take time to find the right balance. Non-hormonal methods, like a copper intrauterine device (IUD), do not affect hormone levels, but they come with their own considerations. The key is to be aware of how hormonal treatments affect attention, mood, and overall well-being.

6. Menopause: Another Major Shift

Menopause marks the end of a woman's reproductive years, usually occurring in the late 40s or 50s. This stage brings a drop in estrogen and progesterone, which can cause hot flashes, mood swings, sleep problems, and other symptoms. For a woman with ADHD, menopause might make her signs more noticeable or harder to manage. If she relied on higher estrogen levels earlier in life to keep ADHD in check, the decline during menopause can leave her feeling more distracted or impulsive.

Menopause can also bring changes in memory. Women might find themselves struggling to recall names or details they once remembered easily. While some level of forgetfulness is common in menopause, a woman with ADHD might find it extra challenging to cope with these added memory problems. She may need to update her organizational strategies or consider talking with a healthcare provider about treatments or therapies.

Hormone replacement therapy (HRT) is sometimes used to manage menopause symptoms. Like birth control, HRT can affect ADHD symptoms in different ways. Some women find relief in mood and focus, while others do not notice a benefit or experience side effects. As always, it is wise to discuss any new treatment with a professional who understands both menopause and ADHD.

---

7. Emotional Impact of Hormone Changes

Beyond the physical changes, hormone shifts also influence emotional well-being. Women with ADHD often have strong emotional reactions, and hormonal fluctuations can heighten these. A rise or fall in estrogen might cause mood swings, leaving a woman feeling fine one day and overwhelmed the next. This can lead to a sense that life is unpredictable or that she cannot trust her own emotions.

These mood swings can affect relationships. Friends, partners, or family might feel confused if a woman goes from calm to upset very quickly. If ADHD is not recognized, both the woman and the people around her might blame her personality or assume she is being dramatic. Learning about the role of hormones can provide a logical reason for these emotional shifts and reduce blame or shame.

It can also help for the woman to have ways to cope when hormones cause emotional turbulence. For instance, she might plan calming activities or give herself more downtime during the part of her cycle when she is most vulnerable to negative moods. Simple things, such as walking outdoors or talking to a supportive friend, can help ease stress. If her feelings become very intense, she might consider speaking with a therapist or counselor.

---

8. **Practical Tips for Managing Hormonal Effects**
- **Keep Track of Patterns**: Writing down daily notes about mood, focus, and physical changes can help spot patterns linked to the monthly cycle or other life stages. By seeing where the difficult days fall, a woman can plan her schedule to allow more rest or fewer demands on those days.
- **Discuss Options with Healthcare Providers**: If a woman is noticing a big impact from hormone changes, talking openly with a doctor can help. She can ask about possible treatments or adjustments in medication. She can also seek referrals to specialists who understand both hormones and ADHD.
- **Adjust Self-Care Routines**: During phases of low estrogen or high stress, it might help to focus on actions that reduce tension. This can include gentle exercise, stretching, or

simple relaxation methods. Good sleep is also crucial, so finding ways to improve rest can ease many ADHD symptoms.
- **Stay Alert for Mood Issues**: If a woman notices signs of depression or severe anxiety, especially during hormonal changes like postpartum or menopause, she should seek professional help. These struggles can be stronger for those who already deal with ADHD. Getting help early can prevent problems from growing worse.
- **Explore Counseling or Support Groups**: Some women find it helpful to talk to a counselor who understands how ADHD and hormones interact. Support groups, whether in-person or online, can also be a place to share experiences and learn strategies. Knowing that others face similar challenges can bring relief.

---

9. Looking at Brain Chemistry More Closely

Estrogen has been linked to the brain chemicals dopamine and serotonin, both of which affect mood and motivation. Dopamine is important for attention and reward, and many ADHD medications aim to make dopamine work better in the brain. When estrogen levels shift, they can alter how dopamine moves through the brain. This is one reason why some women feel that their ADHD medication works better at certain points in their cycle and less so at others.

Recognizing this link might encourage a discussion with a doctor about adjusting medication doses during certain parts of the cycle. Some women, in consultation with their healthcare providers, try slight changes in dosage. Not everyone will need this, but knowing it is an option can be useful. However, any medication changes should always be done under professional supervision to avoid harmful effects.

10. How Hormones Might Hide or Highlight ADHD Symptoms

In some stages of life, hormone changes can mask ADHD. For instance, during pregnancy, a woman might feel more focused due to high estrogen. She could assume her ADHD is gone. Then, once she gives birth and her hormones drop, her ADHD symptoms might return more strongly. This can be a confusing experience if she did not realize that hormones were playing a part.

On the other hand, hormone changes might bring ADHD symptoms to the surface. A woman who had mild signs might suddenly find them much worse when entering menopause. She might have trouble remembering things or lose her temper more often. If she does not link these changes to her dropping estrogen levels, she may feel worried that she is becoming more forgetful or irritable for no reason.

In both cases, being aware of the hormone connection can help women make sense of what is happening. It also provides a way to plan ahead. If a woman knows a certain stage of life or time of the month could be difficult, she can gather tools and support in advance.

---

11. Cultural and Personal Factors

Different cultures have varied attitudes about hormones, periods, and menopause. Some might not talk about these topics openly. Others might provide more community support for pregnant or menopausal women. Personal beliefs also play a role. A woman may feel uncomfortable discussing her hormone-related symptoms with doctors or family members. This might cause her to deal with the effects alone.

If a woman is in an environment where hormone topics are considered private or taboo, she might not realize that her ADHD is affected by these changes. She could think she just needs to "tough it out" rather than seek help. Education and open communication can lower these barriers and encourage women to speak up. Healthcare providers who understand cultural backgrounds can offer more effective guidance, meeting the woman's specific needs and comfort level.

12. Working with Healthcare Professionals

Because hormone levels can shift ADHD symptoms, it is wise for a woman to find a healthcare professional who knows about both conditions. Some primary doctors or nurse practitioners have the knowledge needed, while others might refer the patient to an endocrinologist (a hormone specialist) or a psychiatrist who is familiar with adult ADHD. In some cases, an obstetrician-gynecologist (OB-GYN) might be the main doctor to handle hormone-related issues, especially if the woman is pregnant or dealing with menopause.

Honest communication is key. A woman should share details about her cycle, changes in focus, emotional swings, or any medication concerns. If she is taking ADHD medication, she should let her doctor know about other prescriptions or supplements she uses, since hormones and ADHD meds can interact. By being open, she and her doctor can work together to find a plan that fits her stage of life.

13. The Importance of Self-Awareness and Adaptation

For many women, the best approach is to maintain self-awareness over time. By noticing how ADHD symptoms rise or fall during hormone fluctuations, a woman can adapt her daily habits. She might arrange her most demanding tasks for times of the month when she feels more focused. She could also build in extra rest or self-care when she knows her hormones will cause more mental strain.

In longer transitions, such as pregnancy or menopause, staying in touch with healthcare providers can help a woman adjust her plan as needed. Small changes in medication, routines, or therapy can lessen the impact of hormone shifts. By viewing hormones as a factor rather than a mystery, a woman can avoid feeling powerless. She can try different strategies, track her results, and fine-tune what works best.

---

14. Encouraging Openness and Understanding

It is helpful for women to talk to close friends or family about how hormones affect their ADHD. A supportive partner who understands that there might be harder days each month can be more patient if tasks slip or if moods change. If a woman has children who are old enough to notice her stress, she can offer a simple explanation that some days are tougher because her body feels different. This can help reduce confusion and create a more caring household.

In workplaces or schools, openness might also help. A woman might inform a manager or counselor that she has ADHD and sometimes struggles more at specific points in her cycle. She can request a bit more flexibility or a private space for short breaks. While not everyone is comfortable sharing personal health details, even small hints about needing flexible arrangements can make a difference.

---

15. Moving Forward with Hormone Awareness

Hormones are not the only factor shaping ADHD, but they are an important piece of the puzzle. By seeing how hormone levels affect focus, emotions, and energy, women can better manage their ADHD symptoms. This can mean fewer surprises and less frustration when they realize why some days are better than others. It also allows them to seek targeted support from professionals and loved ones.

The goal is not to remove all the ups and downs of life but to understand them and respond with helpful actions. Tracking changes, trying new strategies, and adjusting routines can help. Whether a woman is in her teens, going through pregnancy, experiencing menopause, or anywhere in between, hormone awareness gives her another tool to handle ADHD with more ease. She can make choices about birth control, mental health care, or lifestyle habits based on what best supports her mind and body.

In the chapters ahead, we will look more deeply at various aspects of life affected by ADHD, including school, work, parenting, relationships, money, and more. Recognizing the role of hormones is only one piece, but it can greatly improve a woman's ability to function day to day. By combining this knowledge with other strategies, women can find ways to stay steady even when their bodies are changing.

Chapter 5: School and Learning

School can feel exciting for some students, but for a girl or woman with ADHD, it can also feel overwhelming. The ways in which teachers present information, assign homework, and grade tests might not match how her mind works. She might have trouble focusing on the teacher's words, or she might get bored quickly and miss important details. Some girls with ADHD are labeled as lazy or careless, even though they might be putting in more effort than others around them. Understanding how ADHD affects school can lead to more effective methods for learning. Below, we will look at different parts of a school experience, from early years to higher levels, and consider ideas that can help manage ADHD in each situation.

---

1. **Early School Years**

In kindergarten and early elementary school, a child with ADHD might have trouble sitting still during circle time, staying on task with art projects, or following multi-step instructions. Teachers may notice that she loses crayons, pencils, or other supplies. She might seem spacey or spend time looking out the window. While some children can get by without too much notice, girls with ADHD may already be forming opinions about themselves. If a teacher scolds them for not focusing, they might think they are "bad" or "dumb." This negative self-view can start early and follow them for years.

Helpful Classroom Supports

- **Clear Directions**: Children with ADHD do best when instructions are simple. A teacher who breaks tasks into small steps can keep a child from feeling overwhelmed. For instance, rather than saying, "Complete these five pages of

math," a teacher could say, "Do page one, then show me before you move on." This helps the child stay on track.
- **Frequent Check-Ins**: Short check-ins can help a child refocus. A teacher might walk by her desk, offer a gentle reminder, or ask a question about her work. This quiet support can gently steer her back to the task without embarrassing her in front of classmates.
- **Learning Through Movement**: Young children often learn better when they can move around. A teacher might encourage them to stand while reading, do quick stretches, or work in different areas of the classroom. This helps a child who feels restless and might lower disruptive fidgeting.

Parental Involvement

Parents or guardians play a big role in the early school years. They can talk to teachers about what works at home. If a child focuses better after short movement breaks, the teacher can try something similar at school. Parents can also help a child plan out homework time by setting a timer for short study segments. Rewarding effort (with praise or small privileges) can help a child see that trying hard has positive results.

---

2. **Middle and High School**

As a girl moves into middle and high school, her workload grows. She might have multiple classes, each with separate homework and project deadlines. Teachers might expect her to organize her time on her own. A girl with ADHD could struggle with note-taking during lectures or forget to turn in completed assignments. In group projects, she might have trouble communicating her ideas or keeping track of her part of the work.

Organizational Tools

- **Planner or Calendar**: A paper planner or a digital calendar on a phone can be useful. She can note down all due dates and test days right away. Every night, she can check what needs to be done for the next day. Creating a regular habit of updating and reviewing the planner can prevent last-minute panic.
- **Color-Coding**: Using color-coded folders or notebooks for different subjects can make it easier to find the right materials quickly. For instance, red could be for math, blue for English, and green for science. This cuts down on time spent searching for papers in a messy backpack or locker.
- **Checklists**: Writing a simple checklist for each class can guide her through tasks step by step. For example, a checklist for an English class might include reading assigned pages, answering questions in a study guide, and reviewing vocabulary words. When she finishes each step, she can mark it off.

Study Strategies

- **Chunking**: Breaking big tasks into smaller pieces helps prevent overload. If she has to write a report, she might first gather resources, then outline the main points, and then write one section at a time. This method keeps her from feeling like it's all too big to handle at once.
- **Active Note-Taking**: Instead of trying to write every word the teacher says, she can learn to pick out key points. She might use bullet points or short phrases. Highlighting or underlining main ideas can also help. Later, she can review these notes, adding details if needed.
- **Memory Aids**: Tools like flashcards, mnemonics (making short phrases or words to help recall facts), or summarizing in her own words can make it easier to remember

information for tests. She could also record herself reading key concepts, then play it back to reinforce learning.
- **Study Partners**: Studying with a friend who is patient and dependable can keep her on track. They can quiz each other, compare notes, and talk through confusing topics together. This social support might also help keep studying less boring.

Managing Deadlines

- **Clear Schedules**: Large projects with far-off deadlines can be hard for a student with ADHD. Marking smaller milestones on a calendar helps her see when each part of the project should be done. This can keep her from rushing everything the night before it's due.
- **Reminder Apps**: Some teens use smartphone apps that send reminders for tasks or due dates. If a project is due in two weeks, she can set an alert that goes off in one week to start the research.
- **Teacher Communication**: Talking openly with teachers can be helpful. If she feels overwhelmed, she might ask for advice on how to tackle an assignment. Some teachers allow extra time or shorter tasks if a student has a recognized need.

---

3. **Social and Emotional Aspects of School**

Middle and high school are also times when friendships and social status become very important. A girl with ADHD may blurt out comments without thinking, interrupt peers, or forget social plans. These challenges can lead to misunderstandings and hurt feelings. She might be teased for her forgetfulness or for acting restless in class.

Self-Esteem

- **Positive Activities**: Encouraging her to join clubs or sports where she can use her interests and energy can boost confidence. For example, if she loves art, an after-school art club can give her a place to shine. Feeling good about her talents can balance out moments when ADHD makes life hard.
- **Support Groups**: Some schools have support groups for students who have similar struggles. Talking with peers who understand can lower feelings of isolation.
- **Counselor Meetings**: A school counselor can help a student handle stress from ADHD. The counselor might teach social skills, time management, or ways to handle conflicts with friends. Regular check-ins can keep small problems from growing.

Handling Bullies or Teasing

Children and teens can be unkind to peers who act differently. A girl with ADHD might be a target if she stands out. Learning how to respond calmly or seek help from an adult can be important. Parents can talk with the school if bullying becomes serious. Sometimes, teachers are unaware of how hurtful teasing can be. It is vital to ensure a safe environment where a student with ADHD can learn without fear.

---

4. **College and Beyond**

For many women, moving to college or other higher education settings is a big change. Suddenly, there may be no parents around to help manage day-to-day tasks. Classes might have fewer checks on homework completion, and professors often expect students to be self-directed. A woman with ADHD can struggle if she does not have structures in place.

Choosing the Right Environment

- **Class Size**: Large lecture halls can be overwhelming for someone who needs more personal interaction. Smaller classes might give her more chances to ask questions or stay engaged.
- **Campus Resources**: Many colleges have disability support services. These offices can offer extended test times, note-taking help, or quiet rooms for exams. Getting registered with such a service can lower stress.
- **Living Arrangements**: Some students with ADHD choose living options with fewer distractions, like dorms that have set quiet hours or a single room. Not everyone can afford a single room, but it can help reduce the noise and chaos that might harm focus.

Time Management in College

- **Set Routines**: With no set school hours each day, a college student can quickly lose track of time. Setting a daily schedule for waking up, eating, studying, and sleeping can create consistency.
- **Use Syllabi**: Professors usually give out a course syllabus with due dates at the start of the term. Plugging all these dates into a calendar as soon as possible makes it easier to plan.
- **Tech Tools**: Alarms, reminder apps, and online to-do lists can keep her aware of approaching deadlines. It might help to set alerts a few days before each due date to prevent last-minute rushing.

Studying Methods

- **Break Up Long Reading Assignments**: College courses often involve lots of reading. Breaking the reading into chunks of 15–20 minutes, followed by a short break, can help maintain focus.
- **Group Study Sessions**: Some students form study groups to discuss lectures, share notes, and keep each other motivated. However, a study group can also become a distraction if it turns into chat sessions. Choosing focused friends is key.
- **Office Hours**: Professors hold office hours so students can ask questions or talk about difficulties. This is a good chance to clarify class material. A woman with ADHD might prepare a short list of questions before going, so she does not forget what she wants to discuss.

Online Learning

Today, online classes are common. They can be a great option for a woman who wants flexible scheduling. But online classes also demand strong self-discipline. Without a set time to attend lectures in person, a student might put off watching recorded lessons or doing online tasks. Breaking these tasks into daily goals can help. Keeping a calendar of when each discussion post, quiz, or assignment is due can ensure everything is turned in on time.

---

5. Testing and Evaluations

Students with ADHD often find tests stressful. They might have studied but then freeze up during the exam, forgetting material they know well. Or they might rush through questions, missing details. Different testing arrangements can help.

- **Extended Time**: If a student has an official ADHD diagnosis, some schools grant extra time. This can reduce the panic of having to finish too quickly.
- **Quiet Rooms**: Taking tests in a small, quiet area can help a student avoid the distractions of a full classroom.
- **Oral Exams**: Some subjects might allow for an oral exam instead of a written one. If a student is better at speaking than writing under pressure, this could be an option, though it depends on the policies of the school.

Preparing for tests often involves repeated review. A woman with ADHD might not learn well by cramming all night before a test. Instead, short, daily review sessions can help move information from short-term to long-term memory. Creating sample questions or using flashcards can make studying more active.

---

6. **Advocating for Accommodations**

Some students worry about asking for help because they fear negative reactions. They might think teachers will see them as weak or lazy. In reality, schools are there to help all students. If a girl or woman has an ADHD diagnosis, she might qualify for special accommodations under laws that protect students with learning or attention problems. These rules vary depending on where you live, but many places have rules that require schools to support students who need it.

- **Individualized Education Programs (IEPs) or 504 Plans**: In some countries, schools create an IEP or 504 Plan to list the support a student with ADHD will receive, such as extra test time or seating near the front of the class.

- **Doctor's Note**: A letter from a psychologist or doctor confirming an ADHD diagnosis can help show the school that accommodations are needed.
- **Follow-Up Meetings**: If accommodations are not working or if new problems arise, it is important to schedule more meetings with school staff to adjust the plan.

---

7. Emotional Support During School Years

Beyond academics, the emotional side of dealing with ADHD can be heavy. A girl might feel anxious about tests or dread going to class if she believes she cannot keep up. She might worry that everyone is smarter than she is. Over time, these feelings can lead to low confidence or even depression if not addressed.

- **Therapy or Counseling**: Seeing a mental health professional can help a student talk through worries and learn coping skills for stress.
- **Peer Mentors**: Some schools have peer mentoring programs, where an older student offers advice to a younger student. Talking to someone who has been through similar challenges can be reassuring.
- **Positive Reinforcement**: Encouragement from teachers, parents, or mentors can boost a student's morale. Recognizing small wins—like handing in homework on time or organizing a backpack—can help her see that she is making progress.

---

8. Transition from High School to College or Work

Graduating from high school is a major step. Some students go straight to college, while others start working. A woman with ADHD might find this change jarring because the familiar routines of high school are gone. If she goes to college, she must manage her classes and living situation more independently. If she begins a job, she might have to handle new tasks without the safety net of teachers or parents.

Planning this transition can reduce stress. High school counselors can offer advice on applications, scholarships, or job options. It can help to visit the colleges she might attend or explore possible workplaces before making a final decision. Talking with friends or relatives about what to expect can also be helpful. If a girl or woman knows that she learns best in smaller settings, she might look for community colleges or specialized training programs rather than a huge university.

---

9. Lifelong Learning

School does not end with a diploma or degree. People learn new skills throughout their lives. A woman with ADHD might take short classes in art, computer skills, or languages as an adult. She might attend seminars for her career. Knowing her best ways to learn—like breaking tasks into small steps, using visuals, or studying with a partner—can help her keep growing her knowledge without becoming overwhelmed.

---

10. Summary of Key Points
- **Early Intervention**: In the early years of schooling, a girl with ADHD can benefit from simple instructions, movement breaks, and supportive teachers.

- **Organization**: Tools like planners, color-coding, and checklists can help middle and high school students stay on top of multiple classes and assignments.
- **Social Challenges**: ADHD can affect friendships. Learning basic social skills, joining positive activities, and seeking help when bullying occurs can protect self-esteem.
- **College Success**: For those who move on to college, using campus resources, setting routines, and choosing smaller classes or supportive environments can make a difference.
- **Accommodations**: Working with schools to receive accommodations can ease pressure on tests, assignments, and daily tasks.
- **Emotional Well-Being**: Therapy, counseling, and mentoring can address the emotional side of ADHD in school.
- **Planning Transitions**: Moving from one phase of education to another, or from high school to work, can be smoother with guidance and self-awareness.
- **Ongoing Growth**: Learning does not stop once formal education ends. Knowledge of personal learning styles and strategies can help throughout life.

By recognizing these points, a student with ADHD can build ways to handle school demands. Though challenges might arise, there are practical supports and approaches that can make academic life more manageable. The aim is not to change who she is, but to give her the right tools and support so she can show her abilities without being held back by ADHD-related struggles.

Chapter 6: Work and Careers

For a woman with ADHD, managing the workplace can feel just as challenging as dealing with school. Work environments often demand punctuality, organization, and the ability to follow through on tasks. Coworkers and bosses might expect a certain level of focus and neatness. If ADHD is unrecognized or poorly managed, a woman might face negative feedback or feel she is always behind. However, with the right strategies, it is possible to do well and even excel in a job setting. This chapter will explore common workplace hurdles for women with ADHD and consider ways to handle them.

---

1. **Choosing a Suitable Career Path**

One of the first challenges is deciding what career path aligns with a woman's interests and abilities. Some women with ADHD do best in jobs that let them move around instead of sitting at a desk all day. Others prefer quieter environments with fewer distractions. There is no one right answer, but thinking about strengths and weaknesses can help steer her toward a better match.

- **Interests and Passions**: It is easier to stay engaged if the job involves subjects or tasks that she truly likes. If she loves helping people, a care-based role might be appealing. If she enjoys working with her hands, a hands-on job may suit her better than office work.
- **Work Environment**: Some workplaces are busy and noisy, such as restaurants or retail stores. Others are more calm, like small offices or research labs. A woman who is sensitive to noise or easily distracted might look for a job with more peace and quiet.
- **Schedule Flexibility**: Some women with ADHD might prefer jobs with flexible hours, allowing them to work during their

most productive times of the day. Others need the structure of a set schedule to keep them on track. Knowing one's personal style is key.

Talking to a career counselor or doing some personality or interest assessments can be useful. These tools do not provide a perfect answer but can give an overview of fields that might be a good fit.

---

2. Handling the Application and Interview Process

Applying for jobs can be tough for anyone, and ADHD can add extra hurdles. Filling out forms, writing cover letters, and keeping track of application deadlines can be hard for a woman who struggles with organization. However, a few steps can make this process smoother.

- **Use Templates**: Having a ready-made resume template can save time. She can customize it for each job, focusing on the skills that best match the job posting.
- **Track Applications**: A simple spreadsheet or list where she notes the company name, the date she applied, and any response she receives can help her remember which positions she has applied for and whether she should follow up.
- **Interview Preparation**: Because impulsive speech can be a concern, practicing interview answers ahead of time can help. She can ask a friend to do a mock interview or record herself responding to common questions. This helps her think through how she will phrase her answers so she does not speak too fast or go off-topic.

Some women wonder if they should mention their ADHD during the interview. This choice varies by individual and workplace. Some prefer to show their strengths first, while others choose to be open if they feel the employer will be supportive. It is a personal decision.

---

3. Creating an Organized Work Routine

Once hired, a woman with ADHD might struggle to keep track of tasks, remember meetings, or manage deadlines. Building a structured routine at work can help. This does not mean she must be rigid every minute of the day, but a bit of planning goes a long way.

- **Morning Check-In**: At the start of each day, she could spend five to ten minutes reviewing her tasks and setting priorities. Writing a to-do list on a sticky note or using a digital planner can guide her actions.
- **Time Blocks**: Dividing the day into blocks of work time can help her focus. For instance, she might decide to spend 30 minutes on checking emails, then 45 minutes on a report. During that time, she minimizes distractions by shutting off notifications or closing unrelated tabs.
- **Regular Breaks**: Taking short breaks every hour or so can help clear the mind and reduce restlessness. She might walk around the office, get a drink of water, or do simple stretches. This can recharge her attention for the next work block.
- **End-of-Day Review**: Before heading home, looking back at what was done and what is still pending can keep tasks from slipping through the cracks. She can note which tasks need attention the next day.

4. **Dealing with Distractions**

Workplaces often have distractions: coworkers chatting, phones ringing, or background noise. A woman with ADHD might find it hard to stay on task when her mind is pulled in many directions. Some ways to limit distractions include:

- **Earbuds or Noise-Canceling Headphones**: Listening to soft music or ambient sounds can block out office noise. However, workplace policies may vary, so she should check if wearing headphones is allowed.
- **Turning Off Notifications**: Constant pop-ups and alerts on computers or phones can derail focus. Turning off non-urgent notifications during important tasks can make a big difference.
- **Setting Boundaries with Coworkers**: If colleagues tend to stop by and chat, she can politely say something like, "I'm on a deadline right now—can we talk later?" Having a signal, such as a closed door or a "busy" sign, can also let others know she needs quiet time.

---

5. **Time Management Tools**

Many women with ADHD battle lateness or struggle to finish projects on schedule. The good news is that there are many methods for managing time at work:

- **Digital Calendars**: Programs like Google Calendar can send email or pop-up reminders before meetings. A woman can color-code different types of tasks to see them at a glance.
- **Task Management Apps**: Apps like Trello or Asana allow users to set due dates, attach files, and move tasks through

different stages of completion. These apps work well for projects that have multiple steps.
- **Alarms and Timers**: Setting an alarm for 5 or 10 minutes before a meeting can prevent tardiness. Using a timer while working on a task can also keep her mindful of how much time is passing.

---

6. **Maintaining Workspace Order**

An uncluttered workspace can help a woman with ADHD stay focused. If her desk is covered in stacks of paper, she might feel distracted or lose important documents. Some steps for staying organized include:

- **Sorting Paperwork**: Having one inbox tray for new papers and one outbox tray for completed items can keep piles from growing. At the end of each day, she can put away or discard papers that are no longer needed.
- **Using Labels**: Labeling folders or storage boxes helps her quickly find what she needs. Clear labeling also reduces the time spent searching for lost items.
- **Going Digital**: If possible, scanning documents and storing them electronically can cut down on clutter. Digital files can be organized in folders, making it easier to locate things with a quick search.

---

7. **Managing Impulsive Speech or Actions**

Some women with ADHD have trouble holding back a comment during a meeting or might interrupt a coworker without meaning to. They might also send emails too quickly. Learning to pause can help avoid regrets:

- **Breathing Techniques**: Before speaking, taking a deep breath can create a small pause to think. This short delay might prevent blurting out an idea that is not fully formed.
- **Drafting Emails**: Instead of hitting send right away, a woman can write an email, save it as a draft, and reread it a few minutes later. This gives a chance to correct spelling, remove extra words, and ensure the tone is appropriate.
- **Meeting Etiquette**: If she knows she tends to interrupt, she might keep a notepad nearby. When she thinks of something to say, she can jot it down first. Then, when there is a proper moment, she can speak.

---

8. **Building Positive Workplace Relationships**

Healthy relationships with coworkers and supervisors are important. Yet ADHD symptoms might cause misunderstandings. For example, if a woman appears to tune out during a discussion, others might think she is not interested. Or if she forgets to follow through on a promise, coworkers might view her as unreliable.

- **Honesty and Communication**: While a woman does not need to share every detail of her ADHD, giving a simple explanation can help. For example, she might say, "I sometimes need reminders, so sending me an email or message is the best way to make sure I don't forget."
- **Being Proactive**: If she knows she might be late on a task, it is better to let people know ahead of time rather than wait until the deadline has passed. This shows respect for her coworkers' time.
- **Offering Help in Return**: A woman with ADHD may have unique strengths, like coming up with fresh ideas or noticing details others miss. By offering her strong skills to coworkers

when they need it, she can build good will. This can balance out moments when she needs their understanding.

9. Asking for Workplace Accommodations

Just as in school, adults with ADHD can often request accommodations under laws in many countries. This might involve flexible hours, a quieter workstation, or written instructions for tasks. Not every employer is knowledgeable about ADHD, but some are happy to help if it leads to a more productive and positive environment.

- **Know Your Rights**: Checking local laws can confirm what accommodations employees are allowed to request.
- **Be Specific**: When talking to a supervisor or human resources, a woman might explain exactly what helps her. Rather than saying, "I can't concentrate," she could say, "Could I move my desk to a quieter corner? It would help me focus better on my reports."
- **Providing Documentation**: Some employers might want a doctor's note or other proof of ADHD. If she has an official diagnosis, getting a letter from a mental health professional can make the process smoother.

10. Balancing Work and Personal Life

Work can drain a woman's mental energy. If she also has a home to manage, children to take care of, or other commitments, life can feel frantic. Setting boundaries can prevent burnout:

- **Setting Clear Work Hours**: If her job allows it, keeping a regular schedule can ensure she is not working late every

night. Once the workday is done, she can switch off work emails or notifications so she can rest.
- **Learning to Say No**: A woman with ADHD might feel guilty turning down requests from coworkers or friends. But taking on too many tasks can lead to chaos. Setting limits is important for mental well-being.
- **Self-Care**: This can include simple actions like reading a good book, listening to music, going for a walk, or spending time with loved ones. Having a few minutes of downtime each day can recharge her mind. If she is feeling especially stressed, a counselor or therapist can provide guidance on how to manage competing demands.

---

11. Handling Stress and Anxiety at Work

Many women with ADHD feel stressed because they are trying very hard to appear organized, on time, and in control. Over time, this can lead to anxiety or burnout. Recognizing the signs is key:

- **Physical Signs**: Headaches, trouble sleeping, or feeling tense can hint at mounting stress.
- **Emotional Signs**: Irritability, sadness, or feeling overwhelmed by small tasks can be signals that anxiety is rising.
- **Seeking Help**: A mental health professional can offer coping methods, such as relaxation exercises or time management techniques. Some workplaces offer employee assistance programs that connect staff with short-term counseling or resources.

12. Exploring Medication or Therapy

If ADHD makes it difficult to handle job tasks, a woman might talk to a doctor about medication options. Many medications can help manage attention and impulsivity. Therapy, like cognitive-behavioral therapy (CBT), can also teach new ways to react to stress and plan tasks. A combination of medication and therapy often works well. However, medication is a personal choice, and not everyone wants or needs it. Each person should consider her medical history and comfort level.

---

13. Leveraging Strengths

It is important to remember that ADHD does not only bring challenges. It can also come with traits that are useful at work. For instance, some women with ADHD are quick problem-solvers. They might see connections that others miss. They can also be energetic, funny, and enthusiastic team members. By focusing on roles that tap into these strengths, a woman can stand out in a positive way.

---

14. Career Growth

Over time, as a woman gains experience in her field, she may want to move up to higher positions or switch paths. ADHD can bring both excitement and worries about new responsibilities. To grow professionally:

- **Seek Mentors**: Finding a mentor in her industry can provide guidance on how to handle larger projects or leadership roles.

- **Keep Learning**: Taking classes or attending workshops can expand her skills. Online courses can be especially handy for flexible learning schedules.
- **Set Clear Goals**: Writing down short-term and long-term career goals can help her see how to reach them step by step.

---

15. Working from Home

With the rise of remote work, many women with ADHD find themselves working from home. This can be helpful because they can shape their environment more. However, it can also lead to procrastination if nobody is around to keep them on track. A few suggestions:

- **Dedicated Workspace**: Setting aside a specific spot in the home for work helps create a mental boundary between work and personal life.
- **Structured Schedule**: Even though she is at home, following a start and end time for work can maintain productivity.
- **Regular Check-Ins**: If she works on a team, setting up short daily video calls or messages with coworkers can keep tasks moving and remind her of deadlines.

---

16. When Things Go Wrong

No matter how prepared a woman is, mistakes happen. She might miss a critical email, forget an appointment with a client, or overlook a major detail in a project. Instead of panicking:

- **Own the Error**: A quick apology and clear plan to fix the mistake can help mend trust. Avoid long excuses; a direct

statement such as, "I'm sorry, I will correct this as soon as possible," is often best.
- **Reflect and Adjust**: After the crisis is resolved, she can think about what led to the mistake. Was it a missing reminder or a chaotic environment? Understanding the cause can help prevent it next time.
- **Move On**: It is easy to dwell on errors, but blaming oneself endlessly does not help. Learning from the slip-up and taking steps to avoid it in the future is more productive.

---

17. Knowing When to Seek New Opportunities

Sometimes a job is simply not the right fit. If the environment is too disorganized or too strict, or if there is no room for personal needs, a woman with ADHD might be happier elsewhere. Watching for signs like constant dread of going to work, extreme stress, or a workplace that will not allow even modest support can indicate it might be time to look for a better match. Everyone deserves a job where they can use their talents and feel respected.

Chapter 7: Organization and Time Management

Organization and time management often feel like uphill battles for women with ADHD. While other people might rely on simple to-do lists or calendars, a woman with ADHD may discover that staying organized and keeping up with schedules requires much more effort. She might have tried different apps or planners, only to abandon them after a few days. Or she may have neat plans but still lose track of time or forget the most urgent tasks. This chapter looks at how ADHD can influence organization and time management and shares ideas for dealing with these challenges in a way that works for each person's unique mind and lifestyle.

---

1. **Why Organization Is Such a Struggle**

A person with ADHD might have many ideas and projects but feel unsure how to organize them. She may also find it tough to choose which task to tackle first. Sometimes, she gets bored quickly and leaves one project behind to start another. Important items such as keys, phone, or wallet may get misplaced because her mind is on other things when she sets them down. Over time, clutter might build up in her space, and she can feel too overwhelmed to sort it.

The ADHD brain can have difficulty with what experts call "executive functions." These functions include planning, organizing, and following through on tasks. When executive function is weaker, it is like trying to pack a suitcase with no sense of order: items get thrown in at random, and it takes much more time and energy to find what you need. For a woman with ADHD, tasks that involve steps, such as sorting papers or rearranging a closet, can feel long and confusing.

Common Organization Roadblocks

- **Lack of Attention to Detail**: Losing track of small but important items or forgetting where objects are placed.
- **Difficulty Sorting**: Deciding what to keep and what to throw away might be hard. She might think, "What if I need this old receipt one day?"
- **Emotional Attachment**: Items sometimes have sentimental value, making it harder to discard them. For example, she might keep old notebooks because they remind her of a certain time.
- **Stopping Halfway**: Starting an organization project with enthusiasm, then losing interest and walking away before it is finished.

---

2. **How Time Management Challenges Emerge**

Time management can be another source of stress. A woman with ADHD might know she needs to leave the house by 8:00 AM, but she underestimates how long it will take to shower, dress, and gather her things. Then she ends up rushing or being late. Or she might plan her day with the best intentions, yet get distracted by a text message or an idea that pops into her head. Before she knows it, an hour has passed, and she is behind schedule.

People with ADHD often deal with "time blindness." This means they may not feel the passage of time in the same way others do. Ten minutes can slip by and feel like just a minute or two. Tasks that they enjoy might cause them to hyperfocus and lose track of everything else. On the other hand, tasks that do not hold their interest might get pushed aside until the deadline is upon them, leading to last-minute chaos.

Frequent Time Management Pitfalls

- **Procrastination**: Putting off tasks that seem dull or confusing.
- **Underestimating Task Length**: Believing something will only take a few minutes, when it actually takes much longer.
- **Difficulty Switching Tasks**: Getting stuck in one activity and forgetting to transition to the next.
- **Lateness**: Arriving late to work, appointments, or social events because of poor planning or losing track of time.

---

3. **Finding an Organizational Method That Fits**

There is no single method that works for everyone, especially for women with ADHD who may have different thinking styles. The first step is to accept that typical suggestions (like "just be more organized") do not address the real problem. A woman needs tools and approaches that adapt to her way of processing information.

Paper vs. Digital Systems

- **Paper Planners**: Some people like writing things down by hand. It can help them remember details better. A paper planner might have daily, weekly, or monthly sections. Color-coding events or tasks with highlighters can make them stand out. However, if a woman often misplaces items, she might lose her paper planner. Keeping it in one predictable spot (like her purse or a desk drawer) can help.
- **Digital Tools**: Others prefer digital calendars or apps that send reminders. For instance, using a phone's calendar app with alerts can ensure she does not forget deadlines or appointments. She could try task-management tools, such as Trello or Todoist, which let her sort tasks into boards or lists

and set due dates. The challenge is to remember to open the app each day. If she forgets, these digital lists will not be much help.

Start Very Simple

One reason organization tools fail is because they are too complicated. A woman might try a fancy planner with many sections or an app that demands many steps, and soon she feels lost. Beginning with something basic—like a single sheet of paper listing today's tasks—can be more manageable. She can expand if she finds it helps, but she should not feel pressured to use all features at once.

---

4. Clearing Physical Clutter

Physical clutter can reflect mental clutter. If a woman's environment is messy, it might distract her from what she needs to focus on. However, clearing it can be a big job. Breaking it down into smaller tasks is key.

Set Small Goals

Instead of deciding to reorganize the whole house in one weekend, it can be better to pick one corner, drawer, or shelf to tackle first. She might spend 15 minutes sorting through papers on the kitchen table. After that, she can stop or continue if she has the energy. Giving herself permission to do a little at a time can keep her from getting overwhelmed.

Use "Keep, Toss, Donate" Bins

When sorting through items, three bins or boxes can help. One is for items she wants to keep, one for trash, and one for donations. Everything she picks up goes into one of these bins. This approach removes the need to make too many decisions all at once. Once she finishes with a small area, she can put the "keep" items in their proper places, throw out the "toss" items, and take the "donate" bin out of her home as soon as possible.

Storage Solutions That Make Sense
She might use clear plastic bins so she can see what is inside without opening them. Labels can also be helpful. For someone with ADHD, "out of sight, out of mind" is a real issue—if she cannot see an item, she might forget she owns it. So, storing frequently used items in clear containers or on open shelves can keep them in sight and in mind.

---

5. Battling Time Blindness

Managing time starts with understanding how long tasks truly take. A woman with ADHD might think doing the dishes takes 5 minutes, but it might actually take 15. One strategy is to time herself doing regular tasks for a few days and write down the results. This gives her a more accurate sense of how long each activity really needs.

Timers and Alerts
Timers can be a big help. A woman can set a timer for each step in a morning routine. For instance, she might allow 15 minutes for breakfast, 10 minutes for getting dressed, and so on. When the timer goes off, it is a signal to move on to the next step. Though it might feel rigid at first, this can train her mind to be more aware of the passing minutes.

Visual Clocks
Visual timers (such as those that show a colored section slowly shrinking) can be even more powerful. A quick glance at a visible clock on her desk might remind her that time is moving, pushing her to stay on task. Some apps also display an on-screen timer in a bright color that fades as time passes.

Chunking Big Tasks

When faced with a large project, it might feel so big that she cannot begin. Breaking it down into chunks that each take about 15–30 minutes can help. If she needs to write a report, she could set smaller goals: pick a topic, gather research, outline points, and write each section separately. By scheduling each chunk in her calendar, she can fight the urge to postpone everything.

---

6. Routines That Simplify Life

Having routines can remove some of the daily guesswork. For example, setting a bedtime and wake-up time helps keep her body in a regular cycle. A morning routine that follows the same order every day—get dressed, eat breakfast, brush teeth, gather work items—can reduce confusion and lateness.

Evening Preparations

To make mornings smoother, she might prepare certain things the night before. Laying out clothes, packing a lunch, and placing keys by the door can save time. By making these steps part of a nightly routine, she does not have to think about them in the morning rush.

Meal Planning

If mealtimes are chaotic, planning meals can reduce stress. She could try a simple approach: pick a few recipes for the week, list the ingredients, and shop once. Then, each day, she knows what she will be cooking without rummaging through the kitchen. Some people find it helpful to cook in bulk and freeze portions. This way, on busy days, there is already something prepared.

---

7. Overcoming Procrastination

Procrastination happens when a woman avoids tasks that feel boring, complicated, or intimidating. She might tell herself she will do it "later," then feel guilty when "later" arrives and nothing is done. This leads to last-minute scrambling or missed deadlines.

Reward Systems
One way to tackle procrastination is to reward herself immediately after finishing a task. For instance, she might promise herself 15 minutes of reading her favorite comic or browsing social media only after she completes an important chore. The reward should be something small and pleasing, so she has a reason to push forward.

The Two-Minute Rule
If a task takes less than two minutes to do, it is best to do it right away. Examples might include sending a quick email reply or putting a dish in the dishwasher. Storing these tiny tasks in her mind for later only clutters her brain. Doing them immediately keeps them from piling up.

Accountability Partners
Some women with ADHD find it useful to have a friend or coworker keep them accountable. They might check in at the start or end of the day to ask about progress. Knowing someone will ask can spark motivation to do the work. This approach can be done with a close friend, a relative, or even an online group.

---

8. Saying "No" to Avoid Overload

When a woman with ADHD says "yes" to every request—whether it is planning a party at work or volunteering in a community event—she risks taking on more than she can handle. This can lead to stress and disorganization.

Learning Limits
She can practice pausing before agreeing to any new commitment. A simple reply like, "Let me check my schedule and get back to you,"

buys time to think realistically about whether she can handle it. If the request does not fit her current workload or energy, it might be better to decline politely.

Turning Down Requests
Declining does not need to be harsh. She can say something like, "I'm sorry, I have other responsibilities right now, so I can't do this." People generally understand that everyone has limits. By protecting her own time, she can be more successful in the tasks she already has.

---

9. Long-Term vs. Short-Term Planning

Some individuals with ADHD find it easier to handle immediate tasks than to plan ahead. But setting longer-term goals or schedules can help her avoid a series of urgent crises.

Weekly Reviews
She might spend some time each Sunday looking at the week ahead. She can note any important appointments, deadlines, or social events. Then, she can plan tasks around these events. This prevents surprises from popping up midweek. During this weekly review, she can also see if she has taken on too many things and may need to move or cancel something.

Monthly or Yearly Outlook
It can help to glance at longer spans of time, too. Perhaps she has a major project at work due in a few months, or a personal goal to learn a new skill. Marking these on a calendar and working backward to plan tasks ensures steady progress. Without this step, she might put them off until the last moment, increasing pressure.

---

10. Managing Household Tasks

Household chores can pile up quickly for someone with ADHD. Laundry, dishes, bills, and cleaning might all demand her attention. Setting a clear structure for these tasks can keep them from becoming overwhelming.

Chore Charts
A simple chart listing weekly chores and who is responsible for each can help keep track of what needs doing. If she lives with family or roommates, sharing chores fairly might reduce her burden. If she lives alone, she might mark specific days for specific tasks (e.g., "Laundry on Tuesday, grocery shopping on Thursday").

Automating Bills
For bills that are due monthly, automatic payments can remove a layer of stress. If she arranges auto-pay through her bank, she might avoid late fees. She can still check her statements regularly, but at least she will not have to remember the payment date each month.

Small Daily Cleaning Bursts
Instead of letting everything accumulate for a big weekly clean, she might spend 10 minutes each day tidying. Wiping kitchen counters, sorting mail, and picking up clutter can keep the mess from growing. Setting a timer for 10 minutes makes it feel more manageable.

---

11. Handling Unexpected Changes

Life rarely goes exactly as planned. A woman with ADHD might find that unexpected calls, emergencies, or changes in routine can throw her organization off. Flexibility is important, but so is having a stable base to return to.

- **Keep Buffer Times**: If she knows she tends to run late, adding a 15-minute buffer before appointments can help. Leaving earlier than needed might reduce stress if there is traffic or any delays.
- **Rescheduling Gracefully**: When an unexpected event forces her to skip a scheduled task, she can pick a new time for it right away instead of letting it float around undone. Putting it back on the calendar ensures it is not forgotten.

12. Using Visual Aids

Visual aids can be great for individuals with ADHD. Seeing a chart, calendar, or list in a prominent place can serve as a constant reminder.

- **Whiteboards**: A large whiteboard in a common area (like the kitchen) can show daily tasks or a weekly plan. She can quickly update it with dry-erase markers.
- **Post-It Notes**: Sticky notes around the house can remind her of key tasks—like "buy milk" or "pay electric bill." However, if too many notes are scattered everywhere, they can become visual clutter, so she should be mindful of how many she places.
- **Color-Coding**: Assigning colors to different types of tasks (like red for urgent work items, green for errands, yellow for personal tasks) can help her brain quickly spot what needs attention.

13. Getting Help from Others

Sometimes, organization and time management can improve with support from a coach, therapist, or assistant. An ADHD coach is someone trained to guide people in creating systems that fit their personality. They can hold the woman accountable and help troubleshoot issues when routines break down. If hiring a coach or professional organizer is not possible, she could enlist a friend who is skilled at organizing.

Therapy or Counseling
Therapists who understand ADHD can help with the emotional side of feeling disorganized, teaching stress-management skills and strategies for building structure. Therapy can also address underlying feelings of shame or low confidence that might stop her from trying new methods.

---

14. Digital Tools and Apps

There are many apps designed to aid organization and productivity. While these can be helpful, a woman with ADHD should be careful not to overload herself with too many new tools at once. Trying out one or two at a time is best.

- **Task Managers**: Apps like Asana, Trello, Todoist, or Microsoft To Do let users create tasks, set deadlines, and track progress.
- **Note-Taking Apps**: Evernote or OneNote can be used to collect ideas, pictures, or reminders all in one digital space.
- **Calendar Apps**: Google Calendar or Apple's Calendar can sync across devices, so she can see appointments on her phone, tablet, or computer.
- **Reminder Apps**: Apps like Due or Remember the Milk specialize in sending repeated reminders until the task is done. This is useful if she tends to dismiss alerts and forget them right away.

The key is to find what fits her daily routines and thinking style. If she tries an app and does not open it for a week, that might signal it is not a good match.

---

15. Avoiding Perfectionism

A woman with ADHD might swing between disorganization and a strong desire to have everything perfect. She might spend hours color-coding files or labeling containers but then give up because it feels impossible to keep it that way. It is important to aim for "good enough" rather than perfect.

- **Aim for Function, Not Perfection**: If her system helps her locate items and remember tasks most of the time, that is a win. It does not need to look perfect or match the neatest examples on the internet.
- **Embrace Imperfection**: She can accept that some days her place might be a bit messy or her schedule might not go as planned. That is normal for anyone, especially for someone with ADHD.

---

16. Gradual Improvement Over Time

Building strong organization and time management skills takes practice. A woman might try new strategies and find they help for a while, then slip up. That does not mean the method is worthless—it might just need tweaking or she might need to refresh her motivation.

- **Look Back to See Progress**: It can be useful to remember how things were before. Has she gone from constant late fees

to only having one late fee this month? That is progress. Has she reduced morning chaos by 50%? That is also progress.
- **Tweak and Refine**: If a certain routine stops working, she can consider why. Maybe her work hours changed, or her personal life got busier. She can adjust her approach to fit the new situation.

---

17. Putting It All Together

Organization and time management are not skills that appear overnight, especially for a woman with ADHD. However, they can improve with the right mindset and consistent effort. Here is a brief outline of steps she can take:

1. **Start Small**: Pick a single area to organize or a single routine to create.
2. **Simplify Tools**: Choose a basic planner or a single app. Use it daily and see if it feels comfortable.
3. **Track How Long Tasks Take**: Get a clear idea of the real time needed, then plan accordingly.
4. **Create Routines**: Develop predictable patterns for morning, evening, and chores.
5. **Use Timers and Visuals**: Keep time visible and break tasks into chunks.
6. **Reward Progress**: Recognize each step forward, no matter how small.
7. **Ask for Help If Needed**: Friends, family, or professionals can offer reminders, motivation, or new ideas.

Through trial and error, she can discover which methods serve her best. The main goal is to reduce stress and chaos so she can direct her energy toward what truly matters in her life, rather than spending all of it trying to fight scattered thoughts and misplaced items.

Chapter 8: Planning, Goals, and Follow-Through

Setting goals and following through can be extra challenging for women with ADHD. They might feel excited about a new plan—whether it is a work project, a personal hobby, or a home renovation—yet they struggle to maintain that effort across days, weeks, or months. Sometimes, the vision is big, but the steps to get there seem unclear. Other times, new ideas pop up and distract them from previous goals. This chapter focuses on how to plan for short- and long-term objectives and, more importantly, how to keep going until those goals are reached.

---

1. **Why Long-Term Goals Can Feel Slippery**

For a woman with ADHD, the future can seem abstract. She might intend to improve her finances or finish writing a book, but without a tangible way to see daily or weekly progress, that dream remains vague. The ADHD mind often responds better to immediate or concrete tasks. Long-term goals can lose their urgency, leading to procrastination or letting them fade away.

Common Obstacles to Reaching Goals

- **Loss of Enthusiasm**: She may start with a burst of energy, then lose interest once the novelty wears off.
- **Changing Priorities**: Because of new ideas or impulses, she might drop one goal and pick up another.
- **Poor Planning**: Without a road map of smaller steps, the big goal might seem impossible to manage.
- **Overwhelm**: She might try to handle too many goals at once, leaving her scattered.

2. **Breaking Goals into Action Steps**

One of the most effective ways to deal with large goals is to break them down. Instead of thinking, "I have to write a 200-page novel," she can think, "I will write one page each day." By turning a big goal into smaller, daily or weekly tasks, she can see progress more clearly.

SMART Goals
Some experts recommend making goals "SMART": Specific, Measurable, Achievable, Relevant, and Time-bound. For someone with ADHD, focusing on clarity can be useful. For example, "I want to get healthier" is too vague. A SMART version might be: "I will walk for 20 minutes every morning for the next month." That is specific, measurable, presumably achievable, and has a clear time frame.

Action List vs. To-Do List
A standard to-do list might include items like "Work on garden." But that is still vague. An action list breaks it down:

1. Buy seeds from the store.
2. Prepare soil in pots.
3. Plant seeds following instructions on the package.
   By detailing the steps, she can see exactly what to do next rather than feeling uncertain.

---

3. **Motivation Hacks for Starting**

Sometimes the hardest part is just getting started. Even if the steps are clear, she might feel stuck. Here are some tricks that can help:

- **Set a "Micro-Goal"**: Promise to work for only five minutes on the task. Once she starts, she might continue naturally after that initial push.

- **Pair a Task with Fun**: If the goal is to exercise, she could watch her favorite TV show while on a stationary bike or listen to upbeat music during a walk.
- **Buddy System**: Doing a task with a friend or in a group can make it more engaging. For instance, if her goal is to read more books, she could join a reading club and share thoughts on each chapter.

---

4. **Creating a Visual Road Map**

Visual aids can keep a long-term goal from vanishing behind everyday tasks. A road map for a big project might look like a line or path that shows each milestone. This can be something she draws on a poster board and hangs in a spot she sees daily, such as her bedroom wall. Each time she completes a milestone, she marks it off or adds a sticker.

Milestones and Checkpoints
Defining milestones helps a woman see progress. For a financial goal like saving $1,000, she might mark every $50 or $100 saved as a checkpoint. Each milestone feels like a small success, fueling her motivation to keep going.

Vision Boards
A vision board is another way to stay focused on what she wants. She might put pictures, words, or symbols of her goals on a board. If her goal is to travel, she could place images of destinations. If it is to finish a creative project, she could post pictures that remind her of the finished result. Looking at this board regularly can remind her why the goal matters.

---

5. **Scheduling Goal-Related Tasks**

A common mistake is treating goal-related tasks as optional extras. For instance, if a woman's goal is to write a screenplay, she might only work on it after she finishes all other tasks. Then she never has time. A better approach is to schedule these tasks in her calendar as if they are appointments. She can pick a time slot—say, 8:00 PM to 9:00 PM—for writing. During that hour, she focuses solely on the screenplay.

Guarding Goal Time
When distractions come up, she can protect that time just as she would protect a doctor's appointment. She might let family members know she should not be disturbed. She can also set her phone to "do not disturb" mode or turn off notifications. By giving goal tasks their own time blocks, she ensures they get attention.

---

6. **Tracking Progress Regularly**

Tracking progress does two things: it reminds her of how far she has come, and it shows where she is falling behind. Women with ADHD might forget past efforts, so having a record can be uplifting.

- **Habit Trackers**: Apps or paper charts that mark each day she completes a certain action. Seeing a streak of checked boxes can be motivating.
- **Reflective Journaling**: Writing a short note at the end of each day or week about what was achieved, what went well, and where improvements are needed.
- **Periodic Reviews**: Scheduling a monthly review where she looks at her milestones, checks what is done, and plans the next steps.

7. **Handling Roadblocks and Slumps**

Any long-term plan will run into roadblocks. A woman with ADHD might feel bored, have a shift in life circumstances, or get stuck on a specific step. That does not mean the goal should be abandoned. Instead, she can adapt or try fresh strategies.

- **Identify the Block**: Is it lack of knowledge? Perhaps she needs to research or ask for help. Is it boredom? Maybe introducing a new element can make it more interesting.
- **Change the Environment**: If she always tries to work on her goal at home but gets distracted, maybe going to a library or coffee shop will help.
- **Short Breaks**: Sometimes stepping away from the goal for a day or two can reset her energy. The key is not to let a short break turn into permanent avoidance.

---

8. **Preventing Too Many Goals at Once**

An ADHD mind might be full of exciting ideas: learning a new language, painting the living room, starting a small business, joining a dance class, and more. While it is good to have a lively imagination, chasing too many goals can cause her to spread herself thin and never finish anything.

Prioritizing
She can ask, "Which goal matters the most right now?" or "Which will have the biggest positive impact?" By ranking goals, she can pick one or two to focus on first, leaving the rest for later. She might keep a "future goals" list, so she does not lose them, but she commits only to the top priorities for now.

Saying No to Self
Setting boundaries is not only about other people's requests. It is

also about controlling her own urge to start new projects. If a new idea comes up while she is still working on another, she can write it down somewhere safe but promise herself to wait before acting on it.

---

9. Using Accountability Groups or Partners

Having someone who expects an update can push her to stay on course. An accountability partner could be a friend with similar goals. They check in weekly, ask about progress, and offer support or suggestions. This could be done through phone calls, texts, or scheduled meetups.

Supportive Communities
Online forums or local groups might exist for people with shared goals—like writing clubs or fitness meetups. When she feels unmotivated, reading about others' progress can spark her own. In turn, she can post about her achievements and get positive feedback.

---

10. Rewarding Milestones

Recognizing each milestone along the way can keep motivation high. Rewards do not have to be big or expensive. They might be something like:

- Watching a favorite movie once she completes a large chunk of a project.
- Treating herself to a relaxing bath or a favorite snack.
- Spending time on a hobby guilt-free.

If she is working toward a health or financial goal, it helps to pick rewards that do not undermine that goal (for example, rewarding a health goal with an unhealthy binge might be counterproductive).

---

11. Developing Grit and Persistence

For a woman with ADHD, setbacks can feel like a sign to quit. She might think, "I missed three writing sessions this week, so this project is doomed." But persistence, often called "grit," is the ability to keep going even after failures.

Learning from Mistakes
If she misses writing sessions, she can ask why. Was it a time-management issue? Did she schedule those sessions too early in the morning when she was not fully awake? Did she forget to set reminders? Each reason might point to a tweak she can make. This approach treats mistakes as information rather than proof of weakness.

Self-Compassion
Being kind to herself during rough patches can help her return to the goal. Instead of calling herself lazy or hopeless, she can say, "I've had a rough week, but I can adjust my plan and keep going." Self-blame often saps motivation, while self-understanding can spark new effort.

---

12. Balancing Short-Term Urgencies vs. Long-Term Vision

Daily tasks like cleaning, paying bills, or dealing with kids can overshadow bigger goals. She might find she never gets to the long-term plan because everyday stuff takes up all her time and energy.

- **Schedule Goal Work First**: If possible, she might do at least some goal-related tasks before diving into routine chores. This can be 30 minutes in the morning or a set hour after dinner. By placing it first, she ensures it does not always get bumped.
- **Multi-Task Wisely**: If her goal is learning a language, she could listen to audio lessons while folding laundry or driving. But caution is needed because multitasking can also reduce focus. She should only combine tasks that do not require the same kind of attention.

13. When to Adjust or Abandon a Goal

Sometimes, a goal might no longer fit her life or priorities. She might realize that what she wanted a year ago is not what she wants now. It is okay to adjust goals if they truly do not align with her current path.

- **Ask Why**: If she considers quitting, does she still care about the outcome? If not, maybe it is best to release the goal and free up her energy for something else.
- **Modify Instead of Quit**: If the goal is too big, she could reduce its scope. For instance, if she wanted to learn an entire new skill in three months, but that seems unrealistic, she could aim for a smaller portion of that skill in the same timeframe.

14. Practical Example: Saving Money

Let's walk through a simple example of planning and follow-through with a money-saving goal. Suppose a woman wants to build an emergency fund of $500. She decides to do this in three months. That means about $167 per month, or about $40 per week.

- **Action Steps**:
    1. Open a separate savings account.
    2. Set up an automatic weekly transfer of $40 from checking to savings.
    3. Track expenses to find where she can cut back.
    4. Plan a small reward each month if she meets her savings target.
- **Progress Tracking**:
  She can note each weekly transfer on a chart. When she sees the balance rising, it gives her a sense of accomplishment. If a week comes where she cannot afford $40, she can adjust the plan or add more the next week.
- **End Result**:
  By following these steps, she might have $500 saved at the end of three months. Achieving that goal can boost her confidence and encourage her to set new financial goals.

---

15. **Practical Example: Writing a Book**

Another example might be writing a short book of 50 pages. She has always wanted to share a story but can never complete it.

- **Break It Down**:
    1. Outline the main plot or structure.
    2. Write one page a day, five days a week. In ten weeks, she will have 50 pages.
    3. Reserve time each evening for writing.
    4. Use a buddy system with a friend who is also working on a creative project.

- **Overcoming Slumps**:
  If she feels bored with the storyline, she can briefly explore a different angle or add a new twist. She might also change the writing environment—try a café, a library, or a porch.
- **Milestones**:
  For each 10 pages finished, she can reward herself in a small way. Knowing a reward awaits can pull her forward when her energy dips.

---

16. **Tools for Follow-Through**
- **Habit-Building Apps**: Some apps turn habit tracking into a game, where you earn points for completing tasks. This extra layer of fun might help keep her on track.
- **Focus Techniques**: The Pomodoro Technique (working for 25 minutes, then taking a 5-minute break) can make tasks less daunting.
- **Public Declarations**: Announcing a goal to friends or on social media can create a sense of commitment because others will ask about her progress.

---

17. **Dealing with Self-Doubt**

Self-doubt can creep in: "I never follow through. I'm just not someone who finishes things." It helps to remember that ADHD is not a lack of ability; it is a difference in brain wiring. Learning how to harness that difference can allow her to reach her goals in a more creative or flexible way.

Positive Self-Talk
Instead of saying "I always give up," she can say, "I've struggled in the past, but I'm learning better ways now." Building a kinder internal voice can lessen the fear of failure.

Chapter 9: Managing Stress and Anxiety

Women with ADHD often experience stress and anxiety for many reasons. They might struggle with unfinished tasks, tight deadlines, or a long list of worries that other people seem to handle more smoothly. Over time, these pressures can build up, making daily life feel tense or nerve-racking. Stress and anxiety are not unusual feelings, but for women with ADHD, they can appear more often and more intensely. The good news is that there are practical ways to address these concerns and create more calm in daily life. This chapter discusses what contributes to stress and anxiety in women with ADHD, and how to handle these problems with clear, step-by-step ideas.

---

1. **Why Stress and Anxiety Are Common in Women with ADHD**
- **Inconsistent Focus**: A person with ADHD may have good focus at some times and very low focus at others. When responsibilities pile up, this uneven focus can make a woman feel like she is always falling behind.
- **Overthinking**: Some women with ADHD have active minds that worry about past errors or future failures. They might play out different scenarios in their thoughts, amplifying worries instead of solving them.
- **Self-Criticism**: Struggles with daily tasks can lead to self-blame. A woman may think, "I should be able to do this," or, "I am letting everyone down." Over time, this self-criticism can feed chronic stress and anxiety.
- **Difficulty with Organization**: Lacking easy-to-use systems for tasks, finances, or schedules can lead to feelings of chaos. Stress arises when important items are lost or deadlines sneak up.

- **Social Pressures**: Women might worry about how others view them. If they are late or forgetful, they might fear that friends or coworkers think they are irresponsible. This pressure can be exhausting.

Stress and anxiety can also show up physically, leading to headaches, muscle tension, or trouble sleeping. Mentally, a woman might feel restless, edgy, or unable to enjoy things she previously liked. Recognizing that ADHD can heighten stress and anxiety is the first step. From there, it becomes easier to see which changes or supports might help the most.

---

2. **Identifying the Triggers**

A "trigger" is anything that sparks stress or anxiety. These triggers can be different for each woman. Identifying them provides a chance to either avoid the trigger or plan a strategy to handle it better.

- **Environmental Triggers**: A noisy, cluttered space might overwhelm someone with ADHD who is already sensitive to distractions.
- **Time Pressure**: Knowing a deadline is around the corner can raise anxiety, especially if a woman has a history of last-minute rushes.
- **Social Events**: Large gatherings or the worry of saying the wrong thing can raise stress levels, especially if impulsivity sometimes leads to awkward moments.
- **Financial Concerns**: Bills, money management, or the fear of overspending can create worry for someone who struggles with organization.
- **Workplace Demands**: A job that requires strict attention to detail or a manager who expects flawless performance can make a woman anxious about letting people down.

A helpful exercise is to keep a short notebook or a note on the phone, writing down moments when stress spikes. Jotting down the situation, location, and feelings can make it clearer which factors commonly set off worry. Once triggers are known, a person can develop specific tactics to address them.

---

3. **Healthy Daily Habits to Lower Stress**

Daily habits can shape how stress and anxiety take hold. While medication and therapy can be important, small lifestyle changes can also build a strong foundation.

- **Sleep Routine**: Poor sleep can worsen stress, making it harder to focus and regulate emotions. Trying to go to bed and wake up at the same time each day is useful. Avoiding bright screens right before bedtime can help the mind settle down.
- **Balanced Nutrition**: Long gaps without food might lead to low energy or irritability. Regular, balanced meals can keep mood more stable. Some women find that keeping healthy snacks at hand avoids sudden hunger that can spark anxiety.
- **Movement**: Gentle activities such as walking, stretching, or dancing can reduce tension in the body. These movements do not have to be long or intense. Even short bursts of activity can refresh the mind.
- **Mindful Breaks**: Setting aside a few moments to breathe deeply or look away from screens can calm racing thoughts. Some people like to step outside and notice their surroundings for a minute or two.
- **Hydration**: Drinking enough water supports focus and well-being. Dehydration can mimic feelings of anxiety or cause headaches.

These habits are not about perfection. Even if a woman cannot do them all every day, picking one or two to focus on can lead to a significant drop in stress over time.

---

4. Practical Techniques for Immediate Calm

When stress or anxiety becomes overwhelming, having a few quick techniques ready can help calm the mind. These methods are small steps that can be done nearly anywhere.

- **Deep Breathing**: Breathing slowly can tell the body that it's safe. For instance, inhaling for a count of four, holding for a moment, then exhaling for a count of four, and repeating.
- **Grounding Exercises**: Looking around and naming five things you see, four things you can touch, three things you can hear, two things you can smell, and one thing you can taste. This helps shift attention to the present moment.
- **Muscle Relaxation**: Clenching and releasing muscles in the feet, then legs, then stomach, and so on, up through the body. This can release built-up tension.
- **Positive Reminders**: Having a short phrase ready, such as, "I can handle this," or, "I only need to do one small step right now," can fight off panicky thoughts.
- **Sensory Tools**: Some people find it soothing to hold a stress ball, rub a smooth stone, or smell a calming scent like lavender oil. These small sensory experiences can break the loop of anxious thoughts.

By practicing these techniques regularly, they may become more effective. It helps to try them during calmer times, so they feel familiar when stress peaks.

5. **Building Better Routines to Reduce Overwhelm**

Stress often grows when tasks pile up, and a woman with ADHD might struggle to stay on top of them all. Creating routines can reduce this sense of overload.

- **Morning Routine**: A short plan for each morning, such as: wake up, make the bed, do a quick stretch, then check the day's schedule. This removes guesswork right after waking up.
- **Work or Study Routine**: Breaking the day into blocks for checking email, working on projects, or taking breaks can lower anxiety about when to do each task.
- **After-Work Wind-Down**: Setting aside 10–15 minutes to tidy up, look at tomorrow's plan, and put away loose items can make the next day feel clearer.
- **Bedtime Routine**: Reducing screen time and doing something relaxing—like reading, listening to soft music, or taking a warm shower—can cue the brain to slow down for sleep.

Routines help lower the mental load. Instead of wondering what to do next, she has a structure that guides her. While routines might seem boring at first, they can actually bring a sense of relief and calm.

---

6. **Handling Overcommitment**

One key source of stress is taking on too much. A woman with ADHD might say yes to extra tasks, volunteering, or social events out of fear of disappointing others or a desire to prove herself. Over time, she can end up juggling more than she can handle.

- **Pause Before Agreeing**: When asked to take on something new, she can say, "Let me think about it and get back to you."

This allows time to check her schedule and energy before committing.
- **Look at the Big Picture**: She might list all her current responsibilities on paper. If she sees she has a big project at work, family events, and personal tasks to manage, she might choose to decline new requests until some of those items are done.
- **Set Boundaries**: Setting boundaries means deciding what she can realistically handle without overwhelming herself. If she must say no, it can be kind but firm: "I appreciate the offer, but I have too much on my plate right now."

By protecting her time, she decreases the chance of feeling stressed by impossible demands. It also leaves room for moments of rest or fun, which can ease anxiety.

---

7. **Learning to Manage Worry Thoughts**

Anxiety often involves "worry thoughts" about things that might happen. These thoughts can spiral and create a state of fear, even if the events never come true. Learning to manage these thoughts can break that cycle.

- **Write Down Worries**: Putting worry thoughts on paper can make them look more manageable. Sometimes they seem smaller once they are written out.
- **Challenge the Thoughts**: Asking, "Is this thought based on real evidence or on fear?" or, "What is the worst that could really happen?" can bring a sense of proportion.
- **Plan Actions**: If a worry is realistic, planning one small step to address it can reduce dread. For instance, if the worry is about an upcoming presentation, she could practice with a friend or look for helpful tips online.

- **Set Worry Time**: Some people assign a short period each day for worrying, such as 10 minutes in the evening. If they start to worry at another time, they tell themselves to wait until the "worry period." This limits how often anxiety interferes with daily tasks.

This approach does not mean ignoring problems. It means giving them proper space and then moving on rather than staying stuck in endless loops of worry.

---

8. Support Systems and Talking It Out

Trying to handle stress and anxiety alone can be tough. It often helps to speak with understanding people who can offer advice or just listen without judgment.

- **Friends or Family**: Sharing worries with someone close can lift some of the burden. They might have fresh ideas or simply provide comfort.
- **Support Groups**: Online or in-person groups for women with ADHD or anxiety can offer a safe space to discuss shared challenges. Hearing others' experiences can ease feelings of isolation.
- **Therapy**: A professional therapist can teach coping methods that are tailored to an individual's needs. Therapies like cognitive-behavioral therapy (CBT) often help people challenge negative thought patterns and develop healthier habits.
- **Counseling at School or Work**: Some schools and workplaces have counselors or employee assistance programs. These professionals can guide individuals through stress management, often at reduced or no cost.

Reaching out for help is not a sign of weakness. It is a step toward regaining balance. A good support system can remind a woman with ADHD that she does not have to solve all her problems alone.

---

9. Professional Help for Anxiety Disorders

Sometimes anxiety becomes so intense and lasting that it meets the criteria for an anxiety disorder. If worry is interfering with work, relationships, or daily functioning, it might be time to see a mental health professional. They can assess whether the anxiety goes beyond ordinary stress and discuss treatment options. Options may include:

- **Cognitive-Behavioral Therapy (CBT)**: Focuses on identifying and changing unhelpful thoughts and behaviors.
- **Medication**: Some doctors may suggest medications that lower anxiety symptoms. These can be short-term or longer-term, depending on the individual's condition.
- **Combined Therapy and Medication**: A combination of therapy sessions and medication often helps some people achieve steadier improvement.
- **Lifestyle Guidance**: Professionals may also advise on exercise routines, sleep habits, and relaxation techniques.

If a woman's anxiety is severe, seeking professional support early can prevent it from getting worse. There is no shame in needing extra help.

10. Using Creative Outlets to Release Tension

Creative activities can be a great outlet for stress. Painting, writing poems, crafting, or playing music can give the mind a break from worries. Women with ADHD might appreciate these activities because they engage their imagination and can be done in small bursts of time.

- **Art Projects**: Simple doodling, coloring books, or painting can help the mind rest. There is no need to be an expert or produce perfect art.
- **Writing or Journaling**: Putting thoughts on paper can be calming. Some people keep a gratitude list, focusing on things that went well each day. Others write freely to let out pent-up emotions.
- **Music and Dance**: Listening to favorite songs, singing along, or dancing around can lower stress hormones in the body. This can be done at home, alone, or in a group.
- **Gardening**: Tending to plants, watering them, and watching them thrive can bring a sense of calm. It also offers light physical movement.

The main idea is to pick an activity that feels natural and enjoyable, without pressure to be perfect. These moments of fun can act like tiny "vacations" for the brain.

---

11. Saying Kind Words to Yourself

Negative self-talk is a main driver of anxiety in women with ADHD. If a woman regularly calls herself lazy or incompetent, she will likely feel constant tension. Shifting toward compassionate self-talk can be challenging at first but pays off over time.

- **Replace Put-Downs**: Each time she notices a self-criticism like "I'm so stupid," she can pause and replace it with, "I made a mistake, but I can learn from this."
- **Acknowledge Small Wins**: If she completes a small task, such as tidying a shelf or making a phone call she was dreading, she can say to herself, "I did what I set out to do."
- **Imagine a Friend**: Sometimes it helps to think, "How would I speak to a friend in the same situation?" She probably would be kinder to a friend than she is to herself.
- **Track the Good**: She might write down two or three positive things she did each day, no matter how small. Over time, this can shift her mindset away from constant criticism.

Being kinder to herself does not mean ignoring problems. It means facing them with gentleness and patience instead of harshness.

---

12. **Relaxation and Rest**

Women with ADHD may feel that they must stay busy all the time to keep up with others. However, never taking a break increases stress. Scheduling short, guilt-free rest periods can actually improve focus and mental health.

- **Short Pauses**: Stepping away from a task for five minutes to sit quietly or get a glass of water can recharge energy.
- **Tech-Free Times**: Constant phone notifications can raise stress. Turning off devices for a set period each day allows the mind to relax.
- **Nature Time**: Going outdoors to a park, yard, or just a quiet sidewalk can lower stress hormones. Looking at trees or the sky helps the mind shift away from worries.
- **Soothing Hobbies**: Activities like simple crafts, puzzle-making, or light reading can serve as restful breaks that still feel mentally engaging.

Allowing downtime might feel strange at first, but it is a necessary part of preventing burnout.

---

13. Planning for Stressful Events

Sometimes, stress or anxiety might be tied to a future event—an exam, a work presentation, or a big family gathering. Planning ahead can lower dread.

- **Step-by-Step Preparation**: Breaking a major event into tasks such as "research main points," "choose outfit," or "plan schedule" can reduce last-minute panic.
- **Practice or Rehearsal**: If an oral presentation is causing fear, practicing in front of a mirror or a trusted friend can build confidence.
- **Backup Plans**: If a woman fears forgetting important materials for a meeting, she might print extra copies or store digital versions on her phone. Having backups can soothe worry about worst-case scenarios.
- **Self-Care Before and After**: Scheduling a relaxing activity (a walk, a warm bath, or a fun chat with a friend) before and after the event can help manage nerves and recover afterward.

With a structured plan, many events that once seemed terrifying become more manageable.

---

14. When Stress Affects Relationships

Stress and anxiety can spill over into how a woman interacts with her spouse, children, or friends. She might become irritable, snap at loved ones, or withdraw from social contacts.

- **Open Communication**: Explaining that stress levels are high can help loved ones understand mood changes. They may offer support or adjust their expectations temporarily.
- **Shared Tasks**: If chores or errands are causing overload, asking a partner, friend, or older child for help can lighten the load.
- **Scheduled Fun**: Spending time doing something pleasant together, like playing a board game or watching a light-hearted show, can ease tension and keep the relationship bonds strong.
- **Apologies**: If she does lose her temper or behave harshly out of stress, a quick apology afterward can mend the moment. Admitting, "I was feeling tense, and I'm sorry," shows she values the relationship.

Recognizing that stress is affecting how she behaves toward others is an important step. With that insight, a woman can take action to repair any hurt feelings and prevent future flare-ups.

---

15. Medication Considerations

In addition to therapy and everyday coping methods, some women with ADHD benefit from medication to address anxiety or to regulate ADHD symptoms in a way that lessens stress. This is a decision best made with a doctor. Possibilities include:

- **ADHD Medications**: Stimulant or non-stimulant medications can improve focus and lessen the stress caused by constant disorganization.
- **Anti-Anxiety Medications**: Certain medications might lower intense feelings of worry or panic. These can be short-acting or long-term solutions, depending on the situation.

- **Adjusting Dosages**: If a woman is already on medication for ADHD or another condition, changes in dosage or type of medication might help reduce side effects that contribute to anxiety.

Medication is not a quick fix, but it can be a part of a bigger plan that includes therapy, routine-building, and other strategies.

16. Recognizing Success and Building On It

Stress and anxiety management is an ongoing process. Even small improvements count. If a woman finds that she can handle a busy day with less panic than before, that is a sign of success. Building on these smaller victories can lead to more confidence. Over time, she may notice that while stress and anxiety still appear, they no longer control her life.

- **Record Improvements**: A short daily or weekly note about what went well can highlight growth.
- **Adapt Methods**: If a method stops helping, it might need a tweak. Life circumstances change, and so do our needs.
- **Stay Open to Learning**: New tools or techniques to handle stress might emerge. Staying curious and willing to try fresh ideas can lead to better coping.

With persistence and a supportive environment, a woman with ADHD can find that stress and anxiety no longer dominate her day. She can explore her interests, connect more easily with friends, and face challenges with greater calm.

Chapter 10: Relationships and Communication

Relationships play a big role in our lives, shaping how we view ourselves and the world around us. For a woman with ADHD, relationships with partners, family, friends, or coworkers can involve extra layers of challenge. ADHD can affect listening, remembering details, or following through on promises. It can also influence emotional responses, which might be more intense than expected. However, these difficulties do not mean a woman with ADHD cannot have strong, supportive connections. In this chapter, we will look at how ADHD can show up in different types of relationships and share ideas for better communication and understanding.

---

1. **How ADHD Affects Communication**
- **Interrupting**: A woman with ADHD might speak up in the middle of someone else's sentence because she fears forgetting her thought. While not meant to be rude, it can still irritate or confuse the person speaking.
- **Wandering Attention**: During a conversation, her mind might drift, making it tough to stay present. She could miss key details or appear uninterested.
- **Impulsive Remarks**: ADHD can prompt her to say something blunt or off-topic if a thought pops into her head. This can lead to awkward moments if the timing is off.
- **Emotional Reactivity**: She might respond with more emotion than the situation calls for, such as laughter, anger, or tears. This intensity can be surprising to others.
- **Forgetting Dates and Details**: If she does not write down a friend's birthday or a scheduled event, she might come across as uncaring, even though she truly values the relationship.

Recognizing these patterns can help a woman with ADHD and the people around her avoid misunderstandings. When both sides know that ADHD is part of the dynamic, they can work together to improve communication.

---

2. Romantic Relationships

Romantic bonds require understanding, empathy, and honest conversation. ADHD can bring unique joys, like spontaneity and creativity, but also certain stress points.

- **Household Roles**: If one partner has ADHD, tasks like paying bills on time or keeping the kitchen in order might feel extra hard. This can lead to arguments if the other partner thinks she is not doing her fair share.
- **Time Management**: Being late for dates or forgetting planned outings can hurt the other partner's feelings or create a sense of being unimportant.
- **Mood Swings**: If emotions swing quickly, it can unsettle the partner, who might not know how to handle these shifts.
- **Distractions**: During deep conversations or intimate moments, the woman's mind might wander, making her seem distant.

Ways to Strengthen the Bond

1. **Open Dialogue**: Talking openly about ADHD symptoms can help a partner understand that forgetfulness is not a personal slight.
2. **Shared Calendar**: Using a joint digital calendar can let both partners see events, reminders, or bills due. This cuts down on last-minute surprises.

3. **Fair Division of Tasks**: A couple might assign chores based on strengths. For example, the partner without ADHD might handle important financial deadlines if that is easier, while the woman with ADHD might manage tasks that fit her energy.
4. **Lighthearted Reminders**: Gentle, humorous ways of reminding each other of tasks can prevent tension. For instance, a simple text reminder about an appointment can save a day from meltdown.
5. **Patience and Reassurance**: If emotions flare, taking a moment to breathe and rest can help both partners calm down before discussing the issue.

A willingness to adapt and communicate can turn potential conflicts into chances for deeper connection. Both partners can benefit from learning about ADHD and how it shapes day-to-day life.

---

3. **Family Relationships**

In families, many different personalities live under one roof, and ADHD can create friction or confusion. A woman with ADHD might struggle to manage responsibilities like laundry, cooking, or keeping track of important documents. Family members could feel they are often picking up the slack or that she is not listening when they talk.

Parent-Child Dynamics

- **Being a Daughter**: A young woman with ADHD may have parents who do not understand her challenges. They might see her as unmotivated or messy. Clear communication and, in some cases, counseling can help families adjust their view.
- **Being a Parent**: A mother with ADHD might find it hard to keep up with her children's schedules, school demands, and

house chores. She might forget to pack lunches or struggle with bedtime routines. Creating simple charts, setting phone alerts, or having a co-parent share duties can relieve some pressure.

Sibling Relationships
Siblings might notice that the sister with ADHD forgets birthdays or does not call back. They might interpret this as disinterest rather than a sign that she struggles with organization or time. Explaining ADHD and making an effort to find solutions—such as setting calendar reminders—can bridge these gaps.

Extended Family
Big family events, like reunions or holiday gatherings, can overwhelm someone with ADHD due to noise or multiple conversations happening at once. Taking short breaks or stepping outside for a breather can help. It might also help to prepare a plan for how long to stay.

---

4. **Friendships**

Friends are often chosen, not assigned, which means they may be more flexible about ADHD differences. Still, misunderstandings can crop up if a friend feels ignored or if the woman with ADHD is routinely late or distracted.

- **Honest Explanations**: A quick conversation that says, "Sometimes I struggle with time and organization because of ADHD, but I really value our time together," can prevent hurt feelings.
- **Adjustments**: Suggesting meetups in quieter spots might make conversations easier. Using phone reminders for hangouts can keep lateness in check.

- **Quick Messages**: If long chats on the phone are tough, sending texts to check in shows that she cares, even if she cannot always commit to long calls.
- **Being Thoughtful in Small Ways**: Women with ADHD might do better with small, spontaneous ways of showing they care—like sending a funny meme or note—rather than waiting for big gestures that they might forget or delay.

Close friends who understand ADHD are usually willing to adapt. It helps to also ask how to meet their needs, so the friendship feels balanced.

---

5. **Communication Skills to Practice**

Improving communication can ease many relationship problems. These basic skills can help a woman with ADHD connect more smoothly with people in her life.

- **Active Listening**: Making eye contact, nodding, or summarizing what the other person said can show that she is engaged. If her mind drifts, it is okay to politely ask the person to repeat something.
- **Pausing Before Speaking**: If interrupting is a habit, she can count to three in her head before responding. Jotting down quick notes can help her remember her point without cutting the other person off.
- **Clarifying Requests**: If someone says, "Please handle this task," she might ask questions like, "When do you need it done?" or, "How will I know I've done it correctly?" This cuts down on confusion.
- **Using "I" Statements**: Instead of saying, "You never listen to me," she might say, "I feel ignored when I speak, and it seems

you are busy. Can we talk when you have time?" This tone can reduce defensiveness and fights.
- **Sticking to One Topic**: If she has multiple concerns, she might handle them one at a time instead of jumping around. This keeps conversations clear.

With practice, these skills become more natural. People in her life may also respond more kindly when they see her trying to communicate in a respectful, organized way.

---

6. **Dealing with Conflict**

Conflict is normal in any relationship, but ADHD-related misunderstandings can add extra tension. A woman might forget an important date, leading to an argument. Or she might lash out under stress. Learning how to handle conflict calmly can stop small issues from growing into major damage.

- **Recognize the Warning Signs**: If she notices a racing heart, loud voice, or an urge to slam doors, it might be time to pause. Stepping away for a brief period can prevent a sudden meltdown.
- **Own the Mistake**: If forgetfulness or impulsivity caused the conflict, admitting it—"I'm sorry I forgot to pick up what you asked for. I understand that caused you trouble"—can soothe the other person's anger.
- **Seek Solutions Together**: Asking, "How can we solve this next time?" shifts focus from blame to fixing the issue. Perhaps setting more reminders or distributing tasks differently is the key.
- **Forgive Quickly**: Holding grudges can build resentment. Once a conflict is resolved, trying not to revisit it over and over can help both sides move on.

It might also help to involve a counselor if conflicts are frequent or intense. An outside perspective can help families or couples learn better ways to communicate.

---

7. Workplace Relationships

Communication with coworkers and bosses can shape a woman's experience at work. If ADHD leads to missed deadlines or disorganized presentations, coworkers might assume she is careless. By addressing challenges openly and using strategies to stay on track, she can build stronger working relationships.

- **Honest (But Selective) Disclosure**: A woman with ADHD may choose to tell her boss or a trusted coworker about her condition, especially if she needs certain accommodations, like flexible deadlines or written instructions.
- **Requesting Clarity**: Asking for instructions in writing can help avoid confusion. If assigned a task verbally, she might restate what she heard to confirm understanding.
- **Using Scheduling Tools**: Shared online calendars, project management apps, and daily checklists can keep her and her team on the same page. This also shows coworkers she is organized in her own way.
- **Being Proactive**: If a deadline might be missed, letting people know ahead of time is far better than surprising them last minute. Offering a backup plan can show responsibility.
- **Team Collaboration**: ADHD can bring creative thinking. Volunteering ideas or new approaches can make her a valuable member of the team, balancing out any issues with organization.

These steps can help foster trust. Coworkers and bosses typically respect someone who is open about their challenges and actively works to meet team goals.

---

8. Social Media and Digital Communication

In the modern world, much of our communication happens online or through text messages. While digital tools can help with organization and reminders, they can also create pitfalls for someone with ADHD.

- **Impulsive Posting**: A woman might share strong opinions or personal details quickly on social media. Later, she might regret oversharing. Taking a moment to think before hitting "post" can prevent awkward situations.
- **Message Overload**: Notifications from multiple apps can overwhelm her, making it hard to keep up with ongoing chats. Turning off non-essential alerts can help her focus on the conversations that matter most.
- **Losing Track of Conversations**: She might respond to a friend's text in her mind but forget to actually type and send the message. Checking message threads at set times each day can help.
- **Online Conflicts**: Conflicts can become more heated online because tone is hard to read. If a discussion gets tense, suggesting a phone call or face-to-face talk might be better.

Digital tools can also help maintain connections if used wisely. Apps that send birthday alerts or reminders can help her keep relationships warm without as much risk of forgetting important dates.

9. **Helping Others Understand**

Sometimes, the woman with ADHD might feel she is always the one adapting or apologizing. She may wish others understood her point of view too.

- **Share Reliable Information**: Suggesting articles or short videos about ADHD can help family or friends learn. This reduces stereotypes or assumptions.
- **Explain Strengths and Weaknesses**: She might say, "I'm great at coming up with new ideas, but I'm bad at remembering times. Could you text me a reminder an hour before we meet?"
- **Remind Them It's Not Personal**: Stressing that forgetfulness or late responses are not signs of disinterest can protect relationships from resentment.
- **Be Open About Methods**: If she is using a planner, a color-coded system, or phone alarms, she can let loved ones know. That way, they see her efforts and understand how to support them.

Healthy relationships involve both sides working together. When people around her see ADHD not as an excuse but as a genuine difference that requires certain steps, they are more likely to cooperate.

---

10. **Couples or Family Therapy**

Therapy is not just for severe issues. Couples or family therapy can help people learn how to communicate, set boundaries, and share responsibilities more effectively. A counselor who understands ADHD can guide everyone in recognizing triggers, patterns, and better habits.

- **Understanding Roles**: Therapy can clarify who does which tasks in the household, how decisions are made, and how everyone's feelings are heard.
- **Problem-Solving as a Team**: With a neutral third person leading, couples or families can brainstorm solutions that make sense for everyone, instead of pointing fingers.
- **Improved Listening Exercises**: A counselor might teach active listening skills or other specific methods that reduce talking over one another.
- **Tools for Conflict**: Learning scripts or steps for resolving disagreements can prevent recurring fights.

Not everyone needs therapy, but it can be a great option if the same problems come up again and again without resolution.

---

11. Balancing Alone Time with Togetherness

Women with ADHD may crave connection while also feeling overwhelmed by too much social interaction. Balancing alone time and time with loved ones can help maintain good relationships without draining mental energy.

- **Setting Time Limits**: If large family events wear her out, she might plan to stay for a few hours instead of the entire day. A polite exit strategy can prevent burnout.
- **Daily Quiet Period**: Scheduling a short period of solitude can recharge an overactive mind. During this time, she can read, take a walk, or simply rest.
- **Communicating Needs**: Letting people know, "I love hanging out, but I need a little quiet time," can help them understand she is not pulling away because she dislikes them.

- **Choosing Activities Wisely**: Instead of going to a loud party, she might suggest meeting a friend at a calm café. That way, the interaction is still meaningful but less draining.

Finding that sweet spot between interaction and rest often boosts the quality of her relationships, as she will be more present and less frazzled when she does connect.

---

12. Handling Emotional Overload

ADHD can involve intense emotions that surge quickly. While these emotions can bring excitement to relationships, they can also lead to conflict if not managed well.

- **Recognize the Build-Up**: If she notices her heart beating faster or her mind racing during a tense conversation, it might be time to pause. A short break can stop an outburst.
- **Self-Soothing Methods**: Deep breathing, stepping out of the room, or focusing on something neutral (like a picture on the wall) can help her regain control of emotions.
- **Talk Later**: If she or the other person is very upset, agreeing to talk again after a cooldown period can lead to better outcomes.
- **Share Feelings Calmly**: Saying, "I feel overwhelmed right now, and I need a moment," can help the other person see that the intensity is real, not a personal attack.

Developing emotional awareness helps in all types of relationships, from casual friendships to close family bonds.

13. Apologies and Forgiveness

No one is perfect, and ADHD can sometimes lead to overlooked responsibilities or poorly timed comments. Apologies are a way to repair relationships, but they must be sincere. A good apology acknowledges what went wrong and tries to make it right. For example, "I'm sorry I forgot about your event. I know you worked hard on it. I'll set a reminder right now for the next one so I don't miss it again."

Similarly, when others apologize to her, it helps if she can forgive them. Holding onto anger or blame can create distance. Forgiveness does not mean ignoring issues, but rather agreeing to move past them once they are addressed.

---

14. Using Strengths in Relationships

ADHD may bring challenges, but it also gives many women strengths that enrich their connections with others:

- **Creativity**: Coming up with unique ideas for dates, family outings, or gifts can keep relationships lively.
- **Spontaneity**: Being open to last-minute fun can break routine and create memorable moments.
- **Kindness**: Many women with ADHD are highly empathetic. They can sense others' feelings and show care in personal ways.
- **Enthusiasm**: Passion for a hobby or topic can be infectious. Sharing that enthusiasm can inspire friends and family.

Focusing on these strengths reminds a woman with ADHD that she has valuable qualities to offer. By balancing those qualities with strategies to handle the tough spots, she can build meaningful, healthy connections.

15. Long-Distance Connections

Maintaining relationships when people do not live close by can be extra challenging if the woman forgets to call or reply to messages. A few tips might help:

- **Scheduled Calls**: Setting up a weekly or monthly time to talk on the phone or video chat makes it a routine, reducing the chance of forgetfulness.
- **Digital Reminders**: Putting birthdays, anniversaries, or other special days on a digital calendar helps her remember to send a card or message.
- **Short Notes**: If long calls feel daunting, sending a brief "Thinking of you" text or voice note can keep connections alive.
- **Sharing Media**: Sending pictures, funny articles, or small updates can keep friends or relatives in the loop without requiring a full conversation every time.

Consistency is often more meaningful than grand gestures. Even quick check-ins can keep a friendship strong across distance.

16. Online Friendships and Support Groups

Some women with ADHD find it easier to connect online, where they can communicate on their own schedule. Support groups for ADHD, mental health, or shared hobbies can be a way to meet people who understand common challenges. However, it is important to maintain healthy boundaries. Sharing personal details should be done with care, especially in public forums. Still, these online spaces can offer friendship, advice, and the comfort of knowing others face similar experiences.

17. Tracking Relationship Tasks

It might sound odd to call tasks in a relationship "chores," but certain responsibilities do exist: remembering birthdays, checking in when someone is sick, or picking up gifts. For a woman with ADHD, using a planner or reminder app for these tasks can be a lifesaver. She can note, "Call Mom on Sunday," or, "Buy friend's gift by Friday." This might feel mechanical at first, but it can save relationships from unintentional neglect.

18. Reflecting on Personal Growth in Relationships

While living with ADHD, a woman may see that her relationships shift over time. Some friendships might fade if the other person is unwilling to accept her needs. Other connections might deepen when people understand her better. It can be helpful to pause and think about which relationships bring peace and support, and which ones cause stress or guilt. This reflection can guide her in deciding where to invest energy.

19. Seeking Joy in Connections

Despite the challenges ADHD brings, relationships can still be sources of joy, laughter, and warmth. By learning communication strategies, setting boundaries, and explaining her needs, a woman with ADHD can build connections that bring out her best self. It might not be simple, but the closeness and understanding that come from sincere effort can make all the difference in feeling seen and valued.

Chapter 11: Health and Self-Care

Taking care of your physical and mental health can be more complicated when you have ADHD. You might already feel swamped by daily tasks, and the idea of adding wellness routines might seem overwhelming. However, simple self-care habits can make a big difference in how you feel. Small changes, done steadily, can support both your mind and body. This chapter focuses on physical health, emotional well-being, and ways to create a self-care plan that suits your own style.

---

1. Why Health and Self-Care Matter

When life feels disorganized, health might be the first thing pushed aside. You could skip meals, lose sleep, or neglect exercise because other demands seem more urgent. Yet this can form a cycle: poor health can worsen ADHD symptoms, which in turn can harm health even more. Breaking that cycle by paying attention to your body and mind can ease stress and boost mood.

- **Better Focus**: Getting enough sleep and regular meals can help with attention during the day.
- **Stable Moods**: Exercise and rest can balance emotions, lowering irritability or emotional swings.
- **Energy Reserves**: With proper care, you are more likely to have the energy to face tasks without feeling drained.
- **Confidence**: Knowing you are doing good things for your body and mind can improve self-esteem.

Self-care does not have to be fancy or expensive. Even simple actions can provide noticeable benefits.

2. Physical Activity for Body and Mind

Exercise is known for helping the body stay fit, but it also improves focus and mood. Women with ADHD might find that physical activity lowers restlessness, eases stress, and promotes clearer thinking. The trick is finding movements you actually enjoy.

2.1 Types of Exercise to Consider

- **Walking**: A simple walk around the neighborhood or in a park can calm the mind. Even 10 or 15 minutes can help.
- **Dancing**: If you enjoy music, dancing in your living room or taking a class can be fun while still getting your heart rate up.
- **Yoga or Stretching**: Slower activities like yoga can enhance flexibility and mindfulness. This may help you feel more grounded and aware of your body.
- **Sports or Group Activities**: Team sports, hiking groups, or workout classes can offer social interaction and structure, which can be helpful if you get bored exercising alone.

2.2 Making Exercise ADHD-Friendly

- **Short Sessions**: Instead of a long workout, try shorter intervals. For example, you could do two or three 10-minute sessions spread throughout the day.
- **Visual Reminders**: Placing sneakers or workout clothes in sight can prompt you to follow through on your plan.
- **Buddy System**: Exercising with a friend can make it more enjoyable and help you stay motivated.
- **Fun Elements**: Listening to upbeat music or watching a show while on a stationary bike can reduce boredom.

Exercise should not feel like a chore. Pick what aligns with your interests so it feels more like a treat than a burden.

3. Nutrition That Supports Focus

Eating well can be difficult when you are juggling many tasks. You might skip meals or grab fast food on the go. But balanced nutrition is key for stable energy and consistent focus.

3.1 Building Easy Meal Plans

- **Simple Breakfasts**: If mornings are hectic, consider quick options like fruit smoothies, yogurt with fruit, or whole-grain toast with peanut butter.
- **Regular Mealtimes**: Scheduling meals or setting reminders can help prevent accidental skipping.
- **Batch Cooking**: Making a big pot of soup, pasta, or rice on the weekend can give you ready meals for the next few days.
- **Healthy Snacks**: Nuts, chopped veggies, cheese sticks, or granola bars can keep your energy up between meals. Store them in easy-to-reach places.

3.2 Nutrients for Brain Health

- **Protein**: Foods like eggs, beans, lean meats, and tofu can help stabilize blood sugar and mood.
- **Complex Carbs**: Whole grains, brown rice, or oats provide steady energy instead of quick spikes.
- **Healthy Fats**: Avocados, nuts, seeds, and certain fish (like salmon) support brain function.
- **Vitamins and Minerals**: Colorful fruits and vegetables offer a variety of vitamins that help the body and mind work at their best.

Try not to feel guilty if you cannot prepare perfect meals all the time. Focus on small changes that are doable in daily life. If your schedule is tight, even adding one more serving of veggies per day or drinking more water is a step in the right direction.

4. The Importance of Sleep

Many adults with ADHD have trouble sleeping. Racing thoughts, restlessness, or disorganized schedules can make bedtime tough. Yet insufficient rest can raise stress, harm focus, and deepen emotional ups and downs.

4.1 Creating a Sleep Routine

- **Set a Bedtime**: Pick a reasonable time to aim for lights out and try to stick to it, even on weekends.
- **Wind-Down Time**: Avoid screens or intense activities before bed. Reading, gentle stretches, or listening to calming music can help you slow down.
- **Limit Caffeine**: Coffee, tea, or energy drinks late in the day can keep you awake longer. Cutting back or having them earlier might help you sleep better.
- **Environment**: Keep your bedroom dark, cool, and quiet if you can. If noise is a problem, consider earplugs or a white noise machine.

4.2 Handling Racing Thoughts

- **Brain Dump**: Writing your worries or tasks on paper can free your mind from holding them in.
- **Gentle Breathing**: Focusing on slow, steady breaths can shift attention away from swirling thoughts.
- **Guided Audio**: Some people use recordings that guide them through relaxation or soothing stories.

Making sleep a priority might feel strange if you are used to late-night work or entertainment. However, the payoff in clearer thinking and calmer moods is often worth the adjustment.

5. Mindful Approaches to Emotional Health

Women with ADHD may feel emotions in strong waves. Joy, sadness, or worry can come quickly and sometimes feel overwhelming. Focusing on mindfulness—paying close attention to the present—can help ease emotional extremes.

5.1 Basic Mindful Techniques

- **Deep Breathing Exercises**: Inhale slowly, pause, and exhale gently. Repeating this can lower physical tension and help the mind feel calmer.
- **Body Scan**: Close your eyes and notice sensations in each part of your body, starting from your toes and moving up to your head. This can ground you in the moment.
- **Mindful Observation**: Pick an object (like a flower or a coffee mug) and spend a minute or two noticing details such as color, shape, and texture. This practice keeps your mind in the here and now.

5.2 Simple Meditation Ideas

- **Guided Apps**: Many phone apps offer short meditations aimed at beginners. They often have sessions of 5–10 minutes, which can be easier for those who struggle with long periods of stillness.
- **Walking Meditation**: If you find sitting still too hard, try a slow walk where you concentrate on the feeling of each step. Notice how your feet connect with the ground.
- **Gratitude Practice**: Taking a few seconds each day to note something you are thankful for can shift focus away from worries or negativity.

Even a couple of minutes of mindfulness or meditation can bring surprising benefits. If you find your thoughts drifting, that is okay—just gently return to the exercise without self-criticism.

6. Relaxation Methods for Busy Days

In a hectic schedule, finding time for yourself can be tough. But quick relaxation breaks may prevent stress from building to a breaking point.

- **Micro-Breaks**: Every hour or so, pause for a minute to stretch your arms, roll your shoulders, or gaze out a window.
- **Relaxing Rituals**: Drinking a cup of herbal tea slowly or lighting a scented candle while you do a task can add calm to daily life.
- **Music Therapy**: Listening to calming music or nature sounds can shift your mood. Headphones can block out distracting noise if you share your living or work space.
- **Progressive Muscle Release**: Tense and release muscle groups, starting at your toes and moving up. This technique only takes a few minutes but can bring big relief.

Think of these methods as small recharges. They do not require a full day off, just a short window where you pay attention to relaxing your body and mind.

7. Building a Self-Care Toolkit

A self-care toolkit is a set of strategies and resources you can rely on when you feel overwhelmed. This is helpful because, in the heat of stress or low mood, it is often hard to think of solutions. If you have a written list or a prepared set of ideas, you can pick one and try it right away.

7.1 Possible Toolkit Items

- **Soothing Items**: A stress ball, soft blanket, or favorite lotion.
- **Fun Distractions**: A quick puzzle or coloring book that takes your mind off worry for a few minutes.
- **Favorite Quotes or Notes**: Jot down encouraging words on index cards to remind you of your strengths.
- **Relaxing Media**: Links to calming music playlists or short, gentle video clips.
- **Support Contacts**: Names and numbers of friends, family, or hotlines you can call for support.

Having these things in one spot—a box, drawer, or folder—can make them easier to find when you need them.

---

8. Creating a Manageable Routine

A routine that flows smoothly can lower the mental clutter that often leads to stress. It does not need to be a strict schedule. Instead, think of it as a roadmap to guide you through the day while leaving room for flexibility.

8.1 Daily and Weekly Routines

- **Morning Check-In**: Spend a few minutes planning the day. Look at your calendar, list the top tasks, and decide when you will fit in basic self-care like meals or breaks.
- **Weekly Overview**: On a set day (like Sunday), glance at the week ahead. Note any deadlines, medical appointments, or social events. Mark when you will buy groceries or do laundry so it does not sneak up on you.

- **Regular Reflection**: Each evening, quickly assess what went well and what was hard that day. This helps spot patterns or problems before they snowball.

8.2 Adapting to Life Changes

Life rarely stays the same for long. If new responsibilities pop up, your routine might need tweaking. Stay open to small adjustments rather than clinging to a plan that no longer fits. For example, if you start a new job with different hours, shift your bedtime routine or meal schedule as needed.

---

9. Mental Health Support

Sometimes self-care and healthy habits alone are not enough, especially if you deal with persistent low mood, high anxiety, or other mental health concerns. Seeking professional help does not mean you have failed. It means you are taking your well-being seriously.

9.1 Therapy

- **Cognitive-Behavioral Therapy (CBT)**: Can help identify unhelpful thought patterns and replace them with more balanced ones.
- **Counseling**: Allows you to talk through problems in a non-judgmental space, learning new coping methods.
- **Group Therapy**: Sharing experiences with others who have similar challenges can offer mutual support and tips.

9.2 Medication

For some women, medication may help with ADHD symptoms or with related conditions like anxiety or depression. Only a qualified professional can decide if this is the right path. It is important to have open communication about side effects and how medication affects your daily life.

10. Addressing Shame and Guilt

Living with ADHD can bring feelings of shame, especially if you blame yourself for not meeting certain standards. This shame might stop you from engaging in self-care because you feel you "do not deserve it" or you "have no time to waste." But self-care is not a luxury—it is a vital part of staying healthy, both physically and mentally.

- **Challenge Negative Self-Talk**: When you catch yourself thinking, "I'm too lazy to exercise," or "I should be working instead of resting," pause and question if that is really true or fair.
- **Focus on Benefits**: Remind yourself that taking a break to move your body or calm your mind will likely make you more effective in the long run.
- **Small Steps First**: If you feel guilty about doing something nice for yourself, start with small actions, like a 5-minute breathing break, and build from there.

Treating yourself kindly is a key part of countering guilt. Each act of self-care can reinforce that you matter and that caring for your own well-being is worthwhile.

11. Making Health and Self-Care Social

Self-care does not always mean being alone. Sometimes involving others can add fun and accountability.

- **Cooking Groups**: Cook with a friend or family member once a week. You can share the tasks and try new recipes that are healthy and easy.
- **Exercise Buddies**: Joining a walking group or workout class can keep you motivated. You might even find new friends who share your exercise interests.
- **Online Communities**: There are many forums where people discuss ADHD-friendly diets, workout tips, or self-care routines. Sharing ideas or successes can encourage you to keep going.
- **Family Support**: If you live with relatives, let them know you are trying to make healthy changes. They might help by reminding you of dinner plans or by respecting your quiet time in the evening.

Being open about your self-care goals can also reduce any embarrassment you might feel. When others see your commitment, they might be more supportive than you expect.

---

12. Handling Setbacks

Everyone has days or weeks when things fall apart. You might skip exercise or forget to take your supplements. You might stay up too late binge-watching a show. Instead of treating these as failures, see them as part of a normal process.

- **Refocus**: Once you notice you have slipped, pick one small step to get back on track. For instance, plan a healthy meal for dinner or go to bed 15 minutes earlier.
- **Learn**: Ask why the slip happened. Were you bored with your workout routine? Did you run out of healthy snacks and fall back on fast food? Figuring out what went wrong can help you adjust.
- **Avoid All-or-Nothing Thinking**: Missing a workout or eating one unhealthy meal does not undo all your progress. Avoid the mindset that everything is ruined. Instead, keep going with your next choice.

Self-care is not about being perfect. It is about treating yourself with enough kindness that you can keep moving forward.

---

13. Balancing Screen Time

Many people with ADHD find screens—TV, computers, smartphones—both helpful and distracting. They can be used for relaxation or to find tips for self-care. But too much screen time, especially late at night, can harm sleep or lead to mindless browsing.

- **Tech Boundaries**: Setting time limits for social media or streaming services can stop hours from slipping away unnoticed.
- **Night Mode**: Many devices have settings that reduce blue light or dim the screen in the evening. This can make it easier to fall asleep later.
- **Productive Apps**: If you are on your phone anyway, consider apps that support health (step counters, meditation guides, water trackers) rather than those that merely keep you scrolling.

Being mindful of how screens affect your mood and time can make a difference in overall wellness.

---

14. Small Achievements

When you reach mini-milestones—like sticking to a sleep schedule for a week or cooking a few healthy dinners—take a moment to acknowledge your effort. This does not have to be a big gesture; it might be as simple as telling yourself, "I did that. Good job." Acknowledging small wins can motivate you to keep building on them.

- **Reflection**: Write down what you have done well this week, no matter how small.
- **Share with Supporters**: If you feel comfortable, tell a friend or family member about your success. Hearing "Well done!" can lift your spirits.
- **Add a Token of Encouragement**: Place a sticker or mark on a calendar each day you complete a positive action. Seeing these marks add up can be motivating.

Recognizing small successes can be a powerful way to fight negative thoughts and remind yourself of how far you have come.

---

15. Staying Flexible

Self-care is not a fixed path; it changes with life's ups and downs. At certain times, you may need more rest, while at others, you might benefit from more movement. Stressful situations might require extra calming routines.

- **Regular Check-Ins**: At least once a month, ask yourself if your health habits need adjusting. Are you bored with your workout? Has your bedtime slipped? Do you need more social connection or more alone time?
- **Try New Ideas**: Keep it interesting by exploring different forms of exercise or relaxation. If yoga becomes stale, try Pilates or a short dance session. If your bedtime routine stops helping, experiment with new methods like reading or a warm bath.
- **Listen to Your Body**: If you feel tired, it might be your body's way of asking for a break. If you are restless, maybe it is time for a brisk walk.

Your mind and body can guide you toward what you need, provided you listen.

---

16. Long-Term Benefits

Sticking with health and self-care practices over time can bring lasting rewards:

- **Improved Attention**: Better physical health often leads to steadier focus, which can help with work, study, or household tasks.
- **Lower Stress**: Regular relaxation and routine reduce the load on your mind, making daily life feel more manageable.
- **Positive Self-Image**: Caring for yourself reinforces that you have worth and deserve kindness. Over time, this can ease shame or negative thoughts.
- **Greater Stability**: While ADHD symptoms may still appear, they might feel less overwhelming when you have strong health routines to lean on.

Chapter 12: Parenting with ADHD

Parenting is a big responsibility that involves patience, planning, and flexibility. It can be both rewarding and challenging—especially when you have ADHD. Your own attention or organization difficulties might become more noticeable as you juggle children's schedules, chores, and emotional needs. Yet, parents with ADHD can also bring creativity, fun, and empathy to the family. In this chapter, we will explore ways to handle the demands of parenting while respecting your own ADHD traits.

---

1. Understanding the Impact of ADHD on Parenting

Many parents feel disorganized at times, but ADHD can magnify these feelings. You might forget an appointment or fail to pack your child's lunch. Mood swings or restless energy can also influence the home atmosphere. Recognizing these patterns is not about blaming yourself but about seeing how ADHD affects daily life.

- **Heightened Overwhelm**: Multiple tasks at once—cooking dinner, helping with homework, keeping an eye on a toddler—can lead to mental overload if you find it hard to switch focus.
- **Impulsive Reactions**: You might respond quickly to a child's misbehavior with anger or frustration, then regret it later.
- **Inconsistent Routines**: ADHD might make it harder to keep bedtime or homework schedules consistent, creating confusion for kids.
- **Emotional Waves**: If you have strong emotional ups and downs, children might feel unsure about what to expect.

However, ADHD can also bring unique strengths:

- **Creativity**: Inventive games, stories, and problem-solving can keep children engaged.
- **High Energy**: You might be active or playful, which can be fun for kids.
- **Empathy**: Having faced focus or emotional issues yourself might make you more understanding of your child's moods.

---

2. Building Structure in Family Life

Children often thrive when they know what to expect. Predictable routines can help them (and you) feel more secure. For a parent with ADHD, structure can be a lifeline to avoid chaos.

2.1 Setting Consistent Routines

- **Morning Schedule**: Have a regular wake-up time, breakfast routine, and step-by-step plan for getting ready. Visual checklists can guide both you and your child.
- **After-School Time**: Decide where backpacks and shoes go, when homework starts, and when play or screen time is allowed.
- **Evening Wind-Down**: Establish a consistent bedtime routine—perhaps bath time, reading together, then lights out. A calm end to the day helps everyone rest better.

2.2 Organizing the Home

- **Central Calendar**: Keep a big calendar in a visible place showing family events, school projects, and appointment times. Use color codes for each child or type of activity.
- **Labeling**: Put labels on bins or shelves to help everyone know where items go. This lowers the risk of losing things.

- **Weekly Planning**: On a specific day (like Sunday), plan meals and check for upcoming school events. If you have ADHD, an alarm or reminder for this weekly planning session can help you remember.

Structures and routines do not have to be rigid, but a basic rhythm can give a sense of order that helps kids feel grounded and helps you stay on track.

---

3. Time Management for Busy Parents

Parenting tasks can pop up quickly: a forgotten permission slip, a last-minute school request, or a meltdown over a lost toy. While you cannot control all surprises, you can practice good time management strategies to lessen the strain.

3.1 Break Tasks into Steps

If you need to pack for a family trip, rather than trying to do it all in one go, split it into smaller tasks:

1. Gather clothes.
2. Pack toiletries.
3. Prepare snacks.
4. Check travel documents or tickets.

Writing these steps in a checklist or app can help you avoid missing anything.

3.2 Use Timers and Alarms

- **Morning Alarms**: One alarm can remind you to wake the children, another to start breakfast, another to leave by a certain time.

- **Task Blocks**: If a chore will take about 20 minutes, set a timer. Knowing you have a set period can help keep focus.
- **Bedtime Alerts**: Set an alarm an hour before bedtime to start the process (tidying up, pajamas, storytime).

3.3 Planning Kid-Free Time

If possible, arrange short windows when someone else can watch the kids or they are occupied in an activity. Use that time for tasks that need your undivided attention—like paying bills, planning the week's schedule, or even taking a quiet break to recharge.

---

4. Communication with Children

Good communication helps children feel safe and understood. But ADHD can sometimes disrupt calm conversation. You might lose focus halfway through a story your child is telling or get distracted by your phone during an important moment.

4.1 Active Listening

- **Face Them**: Give eye contact and put down any distractions.
- **Summarize**: Repeat what your child said. For example, "So you felt upset because your friend ignored you today?"
- **Ask Clarifying Questions**: "How did that make you feel?" or "What do you think you can do next time?"

4.2 Staying Calm During Conflicts

- **Pause and Breathe**: Before reacting if they misbehave, take a deep breath to avoid an impulsive outburst.
- **Explain Feelings**: Rather than yelling, say, "I'm feeling frustrated because the toys are still on the floor. Can we pick them up together?"

- **Consistency in Rules**: If you change rules often, kids may get confused. Try to have clear, simple rules and follow through in a stable way.

Children generally respond well to calm, clear guidance. While perfection is impossible, practicing mindful communication can reduce tense moments.

5. Handling Emotional Swings as a Parent

Your emotional regulation matters. If you have a sudden burst of anger or sadness, it can confuse children who rely on you for stability. The good news is that managing emotions in front of kids can teach them how to handle their own.

- **Name Your Feelings**: Say, "I'm feeling overwhelmed right now. I need a minute." This shows that emotions are normal and can be handled.
- **Model Self-Calming**: Practice what you want your child to learn. Show them that you take deep breaths or step away to gather yourself.
- **Apologize When Needed**: If you do snap, a short apology afterward teaches children that it is okay to make mistakes, and it is good to fix them.
- **Seek Support**: If emotional swings are intense, you might consider therapy or counseling to learn coping strategies.

6. Delegating and Asking for Help

Many parents feel they must do everything. But if ADHD is part of your life, trying to handle every detail alone can create burnout.

Asking for help does not mean you are not a good parent—it can be a wise move.

- **Co-Parenting**: If you have a partner, split tasks based on strengths. If you are good at creating fun learning games, handle that. If your partner is better at paying bills on time, let them manage finances.
- **Extended Family**: Grandparents, aunts, or uncles might be willing to help with carpooling or babysitting occasionally.
- **Friends and Neighbors**: If there is a neighbor who also has children, sharing drop-offs to activities can lighten the load.
- **Support Groups**: Online or local groups for parents with ADHD can offer tips and a sense of community.

Allowing others to assist can free up mental energy, making you more patient and creative with your kids.

---

7. Teaching Children About ADHD

If you are comfortable, explaining your ADHD to your kids in simple terms can help them understand why you sometimes forget things or get overly excited. Use age-appropriate language and reassure them that you love them even when you make mistakes.

- **Simple Explanations**: "My brain works differently, so I sometimes lose track of time or forget stuff. But I'm working on it."
- **Encourage Questions**: Let them ask how it affects daily routines or how they can help.
- **Show Solutions**: If you keep a big calendar or use phone reminders, let them see that you are using tools to stay organized.

This openness can reduce blame or confusion if a plan slips your mind. It also shows kids that it is fine to talk about challenges and find ways to handle them.

8. Fostering Independence in Kids

Being a parent with ADHD can be overwhelming, but it can also motivate you to raise independent kids who help around the house. This eases your load and teaches them life skills.

- **Age-Appropriate Chores**: Even a young child can learn to fold small towels or set the table. Older children can take on more tasks, like vacuuming or sorting laundry.
- **Checklists for Them**: If your child struggles to remember tasks, a simple checklist on the fridge can guide them in tidying their room or completing homework.
- **Positive Reinforcement**: Praise them when they complete tasks. This builds their confidence and encourages a helping attitude.

When children learn how to handle small jobs, it teaches them responsibility and allows you to share the workload.

9. Building Fun into Routines

Your ADHD-driven creativity can actually be a strong point in parenting. Turning chores or tasks into little games can increase cooperation.

- **Cleaning Games**: Play music and have a race to see who can pick up the most toys in one minute.

- **Homework Sessions**: For quick breaks, challenge your child to do five jumping jacks or draw a silly doodle.
- **Daily Surprises**: Slip a funny note into your child's lunchbox or create a secret handshake for bedtime.

These small playful moments break up the monotony and can keep both you and your children engaged.

10. Planning Family Activities without Overwhelm

Planning outings or family events can be stressful if you have trouble organizing details. But with a few tricks, you can still create memorable experiences.

- **Pick Simple Plans**: A local park visit or a short movie night at home can be just as special as a complex trip.
- **Invite Another Adult**: Having another responsible adult can help you keep track of tickets, directions, and times.
- **Use Apps**: Some apps manage travel routes, weather updates, or even packing lists. Explore which might help you keep the day on track.
- **Keep Expectations Realistic**: If your kids are young, scheduling multiple long activities in one day might lead to meltdowns—for them and possibly for you. Pace yourself.

11. Self-Care for Parents

It is easy to forget your own needs when caring for children. But if you run on empty, everything becomes harder. Make time for self-care, even in small ways.

- **Short Breaks**: Ask your partner or a trusted friend to watch the kids for 15 minutes while you do a brief relaxation exercise or enjoy a quiet cup of tea.
- **Nap When Needed**: If you are exhausted, a quick nap can reset your energy for the evening routine.
- **Celebrate Small Wins**: Parenting is tough, so note the moments when things went smoothly—like a morning without tears or a successful homework session.
- **Professional Help**: If stress or anxiety is very high, talking to a counselor can offer coping strategies.

By caring for yourself, you become a calmer, more responsive parent. It is not selfish—it benefits the entire family.

---

12. Managing Technology for Kids and Yourself

In many homes, screens play a big role in entertainment and communication. However, too much screen time can lead to kids being restless or missing out on important activities. Parents with ADHD might also become distracted by social media or games.

- **Set Clear Rules**: Decide on daily or weekly screen limits for your children. Be consistent in applying these rules.
- **Family Tech-Free Time**: Pick a certain hour each evening when all phones, TVs, and tablets go off (including yours). Use that time for board games, reading, or crafts.
- **Self-Checks**: If you find yourself scrolling endlessly, set an alarm to remind yourself to put the phone away. This models good tech habits for your kids.

A balanced approach can let your family enjoy the benefits of technology without letting it take over your attention.

13. When Your Child Has ADHD Too

ADHD can run in families. If your child also has ADHD, you may see similar patterns in them. This can bring extra challenges but also mutual understanding.

- **Shared Strategies**: If you have found success with timers, checklists, or breaks for yourself, involve your child in those same methods. They might help your child stay on task.
- **Understanding Behavior**: You can spot signs that your child is losing focus or becoming overwhelmed, thanks to your own experiences.
- **Professional Support**: A doctor or counselor can provide guidance on medication or therapy for your child, if needed. Family therapy might help everyone learn to communicate better.
- **Stay Positive**: While it can feel tough to manage two ADHD minds under one roof, remember that you have a direct understanding of what they are experiencing. Your empathy can be a powerful tool.

---

14. Discipline and Guidance

Setting limits is part of parenting, but ADHD can make it harder to keep a steady approach. Sometimes you might forget rules you set, or you might hand out harsh consequences on impulse.

- **Clear, Simple Rules**: Post them in a visible spot so you remember them too.
- **Immediate Feedback**: Offer quick praise for good behavior or a clear result for poor behavior. Waiting too long might break the connection between action and consequence.

- **Calm Corrections**: When possible, speak in a steady tone. Yelling can make both you and the child more upset. If you do lose your temper, apologize and move on.
- **Avoid Power Struggles**: If you feel anger rising, take a brief break to cool down. Arguing while you are both upset rarely helps.

Consistency is more important than perfection. Each day, try to handle discipline in a predictable, caring way.

15. Progress

Even small steps forward deserve recognition. If you manage a full week without missing a school pick-up time, acknowledge that. If your child begins putting toys away without being asked every time, that is also progress. These moments build morale and remind you that your efforts are paying off.

- **Positive Talk**: Share with your child, "I noticed you put your dirty dishes in the sink today without a reminder. I appreciate that."
- **Short Rewards**: Small privileges or extra reading time can go a long way in reinforcing good habits.
- **Gratitude Lists**: Teach your children to note what they are thankful for each day. It can be as simple as, "I liked how Mom made pancakes this morning," or, "I'm thankful Dad helped me with homework."

16. Handling Outside Opinions

Some people might not understand ADHD or your parenting style. They might offer unsolicited advice or make judgments. This can feel frustrating, but there are ways to handle it.

- **Polite Boundaries**: If a relative criticizes you, calmly say, "I have a system that works for us right now. Thanks for your concern."
- **Seek Respectful Professionals**: If a teacher or doctor is dismissive about ADHD, consider seeking a second opinion. You want support from those who respect your family's needs.
- **Focus on What Works**: You know your household best. Take the feedback that is helpful and let go of the rest.

Remember, you do not have to prove yourself to everyone. Your primary goal is to keep your family healthy and happy in a way that fits your unique strengths and challenges.

---

17. Looking After Your Relationship with Your Partner

If you have a partner, parenting can strain the relationship if communication breaks down. ADHD traits might add tension if your partner does not understand why you forget certain tasks or get overwhelmed.

- **Regular Check-Ins**: Make time each week to talk about how things are going, rather than waiting for problems to explode.
- **Dividing Tasks Fairly**: If you dislike certain chores, see if your partner can handle them while you pick ones that match your strengths.
- **Date Nights or Quiet Moments**: Even short pockets of alone time can keep the bond alive. Trade babysitting with friends if needed, so both parents can step away occasionally.
- **Couples Counseling**: If communication becomes strained, a counselor can teach methods for working together productively.

A stable, understanding partnership can bring more calm to the home, which benefits children and parents alike.

---

18. Teaching Self-Regulation to Kids

As you learn to regulate your own ADHD symptoms, you can pass those skills to your children. Simple techniques like breathing exercises or writing about feelings can become part of family life.

- **Modeling**: When you feel stressed, say, "I'm going to take five deep breaths to calm down." Children watch and learn more from what you do than what you say.
- **Practice Together**: You can have a short "mindful moment" with your kids each day—closing eyes, relaxing, and focusing on slow breathing.
- **Praise Effort**: If your child tries to calm down instead of throwing a tantrum, notice that effort: "I see you paused and took a breath. That is great control."

As kids grow, these skills can help them face school challenges, peer conflicts, and personal emotions in healthier ways.

Chapter 13: Friendships and Social Life

Friendship can add fun, support, and meaning to life. Yet for many women with ADHD, social situations can feel complicated. From missed messages to feeling shy about personal habits, small obstacles can lead to bigger social issues if left unaddressed. This chapter focuses on navigating friendships and social groups as a woman with ADHD. It explores why some of these relationships might feel tricky, and how to find or keep the connections that enrich your life.

---

1. Why Friendships Can Be Tricky with ADHD

1.1 Distraction and Forgetfulness
A text message might arrive, and in the rush of daily tasks, you promise yourself to reply in a few minutes. But then you never do. Or maybe a friend mentions an upcoming party, and you forget the date. These small slips can leave friends feeling ignored or taken for granted.

1.2 Inconsistent Energy
Some women with ADHD have periods of high excitement where they feel eager to go out and socialize, followed by times of low motivation. Friends might see this as unreliability if they do not know about ADHD's effect on energy levels and mood.

1.3 Impulsive Speech
Blurting out a personal secret or interrupting mid-conversation can push friends away if they feel disrespected. Though these moments are not meant to be rude, repeated impulsivity might strain the connection.

1.4 Sensitivity to Criticism
Women with ADHD might overthink a friend's comment or feel deeply hurt by minor conflicts. Worrying about what others think can make socializing feel like tiptoeing on eggshells.

Knowing these patterns can help you notice them early and avoid turning small missteps into big rifts. Good friends usually adjust when they understand what is going on. But that requires a willingness to talk openly about your needs and challenges.

---

2. Finding Your Social Comfort Zone

2.1 Understanding Your Social Style
You might be more introverted, preferring smaller groups or one-on-one time. Or you could be very outgoing, enjoying large gatherings but losing track of deeper connections. Recognizing how you best interact helps you choose social situations that suit you.

- **Small Groups**: If big parties are overwhelming, you could suggest meeting friends in more intimate settings like cafés or at home.
- **Structured Events**: Some people with ADHD prefer events with activities—board games, crafts, or group walks—because there is a built-in focus instead of unstructured mingling.

2.2 Setting Realistic Expectations
You do not have to be everyone's best friend or go to every social event. Figure out how much social time feels good without wearing you down. If you thrive on weekly get-togethers but feel stressed by multiple outings in a few days, plan accordingly. Protecting your mental energy can keep friendships healthy rather than forcing yourself into exhaustion.

3. Making New Friends

3.1 Overcoming Social Anxiety
If you worry about making a poor impression, remind yourself that many people appreciate authenticity over perfection. Small slip-ups are common for everyone, not just those with ADHD. You can start with polite conversation and see if there is a shared interest that might bond you. If you do interrupt or forget something, a sincere "I'm sorry—I didn't mean to cut you off" can fix the moment.

3.2 Joining Groups and Communities
Local clubs, hobby meetups, or online groups can introduce you to new friends who share your passions—whether it is reading, gardening, volunteering, or any other activity. A structured setting can help reduce the pressure of making conversation from scratch.

- **Hobby Classes**: Cooking lessons, painting workshops, or dance sessions can bring people together for shared learning.
- **Community Events**: Local libraries, community centers, or sports clubs often host free or low-cost gatherings.
- **Online Platforms**: If in-person meetings are not accessible, online communities allow you to chat with people across the globe. Some ADHD-focused forums might also help you find those who truly understand your daily hurdles.

3.3 Being Approachable
A friendly smile or a simple greeting can open doors. If you appear tense, people may assume you prefer to be left alone. Small gestures—like offering to share your pen, or asking a person how they found the event—can break the ice in a gentle way.

4. Nurturing Existing Friendships

4.1 Staying in Touch
ADHD can make it hard to keep consistent contact. Still, quick efforts can maintain the bond:

- **Set Reminders**: Use phone alerts to prompt you to check in with friends you have not contacted recently. A short text or voice note can show you care, even if you are busy.
- **Digital Tools**: Calendar apps can help you note friends' birthdays or important milestones. This is especially helpful if you often forget dates.
- **Honesty about Delays**: If you have not replied for a while, a short explanation—"I got sidetracked, but I was thinking about you"—goes a long way.

4.2 Handling Conflict Carefully
Every friendship can hit bumps. If a friend seems distant or upset:

- **Ask Directly**: "I sense something might be off—did I do something that bothered you?"
- **Listen Attentively**: Resist the urge to defend yourself right away; hear them out. This helps you see the situation from their view.
- **Apologize Sincerely**: If your ADHD habits caused an issue, own it. Show willingness to make changes, like setting more reliable reminders or being more mindful when talking.
- **Set Boundaries**: If a friend constantly criticizes or belittles your ADHD traits, decide if this is healthy for you. Real friends aim to understand, not shame.

4.3 Balancing Old and New Connections
A big social circle can be overwhelming to manage if ADHD makes your life already full of tasks. It is okay to have a few close friends and some casual acquaintances. Choose the relationships that truly

bring joy and support rather than trying to hold onto every connection out of guilt.

5. Supporting Friends While Handling ADHD

5.1 Being There for Others
Friendship is not only about receiving support but also giving it. Despite ADHD, you can still be an empathetic listener or offer thoughtful advice. Even if you sometimes forget details, try to remember the main points your friend shared. If memory is an issue, jot down a quick note after a chat: "Jane's cat is sick," or "Tom is worried about his job interview." Reviewing these notes next time you speak can show you truly care.

5.2 Avoiding Overcommitment
It is tempting to say yes to every favor or invitation so you do not disappoint anyone. But taking on too much can backfire if ADHD leaves you stretched thin. Politely explain, "I really want to help, but my schedule is tight right now. Can we find another way?" This approach respects both your friend's need and your personal limits.

5.3 Communicating Your Needs
If impulsivity or distraction is common for you, let friends know the best ways to keep you engaged. Ask them to text you reminders about a planned hangout or to gently let you know if you are talking too fast. Many friends are happy to accommodate once they understand how ADHD affects you.

6. Handling Social Events

6.1 Large Gatherings
Whether it is a wedding, a big party, or a community fair, these

events can overstimulate someone with ADHD. The noise, conversations, and unpredictability can lead to restlessness.

- **Plan an Escape Hatch**: Decide beforehand how long you plan to stay. Keep a backup plan in case you feel overwhelmed—maybe step outside to breathe or leave earlier than others.
- **Focus on Small Groups**: Instead of mingling with everyone at once, chat with one or two people at a time. This can reduce mental overload.
- **Use a Buddy**: If a close friend is also attending, let them know you might need breaks or quieter spots during the event.

6.2 Setting Boundaries on Social Media
Online interactions can add a layer of social complexity. Constant notifications might distract you from real-life tasks, causing more stress. Try limiting your social media checks to certain times of day. Turn off unneeded alerts. Friends who interact mostly online might need to know you do not respond to messages right away.

---

7. Dealing with Rejection or Friendship Loss

7.1 Not Everyone Will Get It
Sometimes, you might connect with someone who cannot handle ADHD quirks. They might see your forgetfulness as laziness or your impulsiveness as rudeness. While it stings, understand that not every person will be a match. That is part of life, with or without ADHD.

7.2 Coping with Disappointment
Losing a friend or facing rejection can feel very personal. It is normal to grieve a lost connection. If blame or self-criticism creeps in—"I messed up again"—remind yourself that relationships end for many

reasons, and ADHD is just one factor. Talking to a supportive person or counselor can help you move forward.

7.3 Learning from the Experience
Look at what happened. Did the friendship fail because of repeated missed plans? Or was it miscommunication about expectations? If there is a pattern, see if you can tweak your approach. This might mean scheduling fewer but more solid plans or practicing listening skills more carefully.

---

8. Social Self-Care

8.1 Pacing Your Social Life
If you are highly social, you might stretch yourself thin by attending multiple gatherings back-to-back. Or if you are less social, you might isolate yourself for weeks. Aim for balance: enjoy time with friends, but also schedule downtime to recharge, especially if ADHD tasks demand lots of mental energy.

8.2 Emotional Boundaries
Friends can be wonderful but also overwhelming if they rely on you too heavily. If a friend often vents their problems for hours, draining your emotional reserves, kindly set limits. "I'm here for you, but could we talk about a few solutions? I have to manage my own stress, too."

8.3 Small Wins in Friendship
When you manage to follow through on a social plan or navigate a tough conversation calmly, take a moment to recognize that. It might sound minor to others, but for someone with ADHD, these successes are meaningful. Giving yourself credit for these efforts can boost your self-worth and keep you motivated to keep nurturing friendships.

9. What If Friends Are Far Away?

9.1 Long-Distance Bonds
Technology helps keep connections alive even if friends live across the country. Schedule video calls or send voice messages. Remember to keep track of time zones if relevant.

9.2 Sending Small Surprises
A funny meme, a digital card, or a care package can remind a friend you are thinking of them. If you worry about forgetting, set a calendar reminder for special occasions like birthdays or major life events.

9.3 Online Friendships
If you find it challenging to form local friendships due to your work schedule or location, online communities can fill part of the gap. It is good to be cautious with personal information, but lasting bonds can develop in shared-interest groups or forums.

10. Embracing Who You Are

10.1 Authenticity vs. People-Pleasing
Some women with ADHD try to hide their traits to "fit in," such as forcing themselves to be quieter than they naturally are, or pretending not to have forgetful moments. While polite adjustments are fine, ignoring who you are can lead to feeling lonely even in a crowd. True friendship flourishes when you can be yourself—forgetful moments, impulsive jokes, and all—and still feel accepted.

10.2 Owning Your Strengths

ADHD can make you lively, quick-witted, and enthusiastic. You might be the one who suggests spontaneous adventures or helps friends see an issue from a fresh angle. Celebrate these aspects instead of focusing only on the difficult parts.

10.3 Encouraging Self-Compassion

Social struggles do not define your worth. If you realize you forgot a friend's birthday or accidentally cut someone off in conversation, handle it with self-kindness. Apologize or correct it, then move on. Belaboring the mistake only creates more anxiety and might make you avoid socializing.

---

11. Building a Supportive Circle

11.1 Seek Out People Who Understand

Connecting with others who have ADHD or those who respect it can lessen the pressure to be "perfect." They are more likely to forgive late replies or occasional changes in plans without taking it personally.

11.2 Family-Like Friendships

Close friends can act like chosen family. If you do not have strong support from relatives, these friend relationships may be vital for emotional support. Keep these ties strong by communicating openly and being there in return when they need you.

11.3 Mentors or Guides

Sometimes, it helps to have older or more experienced friends who can give advice on social scenarios or personal growth. A mentor figure can guide you through tricky situations, such as dealing with coworker conflicts or planning a big social event. This guidance can ease stress and help you develop social confidence.

12. Addressing Loneliness

12.1 Recognizing the Feeling
Loneliness can creep in if you isolate yourself due to shame or if life changes (like moving to a new city or changing jobs) reduce your connections. Feeling lonely is not a personal failing—it is a signal that you might benefit from more social or emotional contact.

12.2 Practical Steps to Combat Isolation

- **Join Community Efforts**: Volunteering for a local charity or event can give you a sense of purpose and a chance to meet like-minded people.
- **Set Small Goals**: If you have not socialized in a while, commit to inviting one friend out for coffee this month or attending one group activity.
- **Therapy or Counseling**: A mental health professional can help you handle feelings of loneliness, especially if they are tied to self-doubt or past social pain.

12.3 Digital Connections
When in-person options feel intimidating, online or phone-based friendships are still valid. You can find support groups for women with ADHD, chat with people who share your hobbies, or even arrange virtual watch parties for movies. Just be sure to keep a healthy balance and not rely solely on screens for all social needs.

Chapter 14: Self-Confidence and Self-Esteem

Feeling good about yourself can help you face daily challenges with resilience. Yet many women with ADHD struggle to trust their own abilities. Early life experiences—like being called "lazy" or "scatterbrained"—may have chipped away at self-esteem. Even in adulthood, daily missteps can reinforce the idea that "I'm not good enough." This chapter explores ways to build a healthier sense of self so you can move forward with optimism and strength.

---

1. What Shapes Self-Confidence?

1.1 Personal History
Comments from parents, teachers, or peers stick with us. If you heard criticisms about daydreaming, tardiness, or lack of organization, those messages might linger. Over time, you may have internalized negative beliefs about your capabilities.

1.2 Ongoing Challenges
Women with ADHD often juggle responsibilities that feel heavier due to attention or memory struggles. Forgetting an appointment or missing a deadline can trigger self-blame, reinforcing the notion that you cannot handle things. This cycle can erode self-confidence.

1.3 Societal Pressures
Expectations for women—like being perfectly organized, nurturing, and always on top of tasks—can feel impossible if your ADHD makes certain duties extra tough. Comparing yourself to an ideal can worsen self-doubt.

Breaking free of these influences starts with recognizing them. Understanding that your current self-image did not arise from nowhere, but from specific experiences, can help you dismantle unhelpful beliefs.

---

2. Recognizing Negative Thought Patterns

2.1 Black-and-White Thinking
You might see outcomes as total success or total failure. If you did not complete every single step perfectly, you think you bombed it. This ignores all the partial achievements and improvements along the way.

2.2 Overgeneralizing
One slip-up—like missing one day of exercise—turns into "I always fail at routines." This broad statement is rarely true but can feel convincing in the moment.

2.3 Personalizing
If a coworker is short-tempered, you might assume it is your fault. In reality, they may have had a bad morning or faced unrelated stress. Yet personalizing means you automatically blame yourself.

2.4 "Should" Statements
Phrases like "I should be able to do this without help" or "I shouldn't ever make silly mistakes" create rigid rules that do not respect your ADHD reality. They turn normal human slip-ups into major self-judgments.

Spotting these patterns is half the battle. Whenever a negative thought pops up, you can test it: "Is it true? Is there another explanation?" Over time, you learn to replace harsh self-talk with more balanced perspectives.

---

3. Strategies to Boost Self-Worth

3.1 Focusing on Strengths First
If ADHD traits dominate your self-image, you may forget your natural gifts. List out qualities or skills you are proud of, such as creativity, kindness, humor, or problem-solving. Keep this list somewhere visible. When you start doubting yourself, look at the list to recall your positive traits.

3.2 Setting Achievable Goals
Huge goals like "become super organized overnight" can lead to frustration. Instead, choose small, concrete targets. For example, aim to keep your car keys in the same spot every day or to finish reading one book chapter each week. Achieving these modest goals can give you steady confidence boosts.

---

4. Self-Talk Makeover

4.1 Confronting Inner Criticism
When you hear your inner voice saying, "I messed everything up," pause. Ask yourself:

- **Is it really "everything"?** Maybe you missed one step, but other parts of the task were fine.
- **What can I learn?** Instead of labeling yourself as incompetent, treat the moment as feedback for next time.

4.2 Using Gentle Phrases
Swap harsh phrases—"I'm so stupid"—with gentle, fact-based statements: "I made a mistake, but I can fix it," or "I'm learning to manage my time better." These small changes in wording can gradually reshape how you see yourself.

4.3 Humor and Self-Compassion

Sometimes, having a sense of humor about ADHD slip-ups helps defuse tension. A small laugh at a silly oversight can calm the sting of embarrassment. Pair humor with self-compassion: "It's just an error; I'll try a different approach next time." Overly harsh reactions harm self-esteem, while a soft chuckle can keep a balanced perspective.

---

5. Body Confidence and Physical Self-Esteem

5.1 ADHD, Body Image, and Habits

If ADHD affects your eating habits or exercise routines, you might feel less confident about your health or appearance. Maybe you get hyperfocused on certain tasks and forget to eat balanced meals, or you struggle to maintain a workout plan. Understanding how ADHD impacts these routines can help you set realistic goals without blaming yourself.

5.2 Dressing with Ease

Looking good can boost self-esteem, but maintaining a neat wardrobe can be tough if you misplace clothes or forget to do laundry. One solution is to keep a smaller, well-organized set of outfits that you really like, rather than a huge messy closet. This can reduce decision fatigue and help you feel more in control of your appearance.

5.3 Physical Health Ups Self-Worth

We have covered health and self-care, but it is worth repeating: exercising in a way you enjoy, eating nutritiously, and getting enough rest can sharpen the mind and create a positive body-mind loop. Feeling good physically can feed into feeling good mentally.

6. Comparing Yourself to Others

6.1 The Comparison Trap
It is tempting to see someone with a perfectly tidy house or an impressive career and think, "I'm so behind." But you do not see that person's private struggles. Everyone's life has challenges, many of which are hidden.

6.2 Social Media Illusions
On social platforms, people often showcase their best moments. If you are struggling with ADHD management while scrolling through photos of pristine kitchens or elaborate events, you might feel inadequate. Remind yourself that images online are curated, not full reality.

6.3 Competing Only with Your Past Self
Rather than measuring yourself against another person, look at where you were six months or a year ago. Have you improved your time management skills, even slightly? Have you learned new ways to handle stress? Tracking personal growth is more motivating and fair than comparing with others whose circumstances may differ drastically from yours.

---

7. Handling External Criticism

7.1 Dealing with Unwanted Opinions
Friends, family, or coworkers may offer remarks like "Why don't you just try harder?" If you already struggle with self-esteem, these comments can sting. Decide which feedback might be useful and which is simply unhelpful. It is okay to politely set boundaries when someone repeatedly tears you down.

7.2 Overcoming Workplace Doubt

In professional settings, if a boss or coworker questions your ability, consider calmly presenting your strengths and strategies. For instance, "I use this task-management app to ensure deadlines are met, and it has been working well. Let me show you the progress I've made." Showcasing practical solutions can counter negative assumptions.

7.3 Finding Safe People

Look for those in your circle who offer respect and encouragement. This does not mean surrounding yourself with yes-people, but rather seeking balanced, constructive views that help you grow rather than undermine your confidence.

---

8. Activities that Build Self-Esteem

8.1 Learning New Skills

Taking on a new hobby or skill can remind you that you are capable of mastering fresh challenges. Whether it is learning a new language, trying a craft, or mastering a simple recipe, each step forward can spark self-pride. If ADHD makes it tricky, break the learning process into small, achievable segments.

8.2 Creative Outlets

Painting, writing, singing—any creative activity can be a way to express feelings and discover talents. You do not need to be a pro to find fulfillment in creativity. Overcoming the worry of "I'm not good enough at this" and simply enjoying the process can raise your sense of competence.

8.3 Volunteering or Helping Others

Sometimes, shifting the focus from your own struggles to helping someone else can lift your self-esteem. Volunteering at a shelter, tutoring kids, or assisting neighbors fosters a sense of purpose. You realize you have value to offer, which can quiet the negative voices in your head.

---

9. Reframing Failures

9.1 Seeing Mistakes as Lessons
Instead of labeling a mistake as proof of incompetence, ask, "What can I learn here?" Maybe you realize you need a better reminder system, or that you do better with tasks when you do them earlier in the day. Turning failures into insights gives them a positive spin.

9.2 Adjusting Expectations
If your list of tasks each day is too long, you set yourself up for defeat. Lowering the number of tasks to what is realistically doable leaves space for success. Meeting a few goals consistently often feels better than half-finishing a long list that was never practical.

9.3 Forgiving Yourself Quickly
Lingering on guilt or shame drains mental energy. Practice a quick apology if needed—like telling a friend you are sorry for missing a call—then move on. Replaying the mistake repeatedly will not fix it and will only erode your self-esteem further.

---

10. Support Systems for Self-Confidence

10.1 Therapy
A counselor or therapist can guide you through self-esteem struggles, helping you identify harmful thought patterns and offering tools to reshape them. Therapies like cognitive-behavioral

therapy (CBT) can be especially helpful for challenging negative beliefs.

10.2 Mentors and Role Models
Look for people who have faced similar struggles but thrived. This could be someone in your personal life or a public figure with ADHD. Seeing their journey (without using that disallowed term in writing) might inspire you to realize you are not alone, and success is possible.

10.3 ADHD Support Groups
Online or local meetups let you connect with others who understand your experiences. Sharing stories of triumphs and setbacks can normalize what you are going through and offer fresh ideas for boosting self-esteem.

---

11. Mindset Shifts for Lasting Confidence

11.1 Emphasizing Progress over Perfection
Perfectionism often sinks self-esteem. Learning to appreciate small gains—a better handle on your budget, a neater workspace—can help you see that improvement is ongoing and valuable.

11.2 Embracing Setbacks
Sometimes you will slip. Self-confidence does not mean never failing; it means you trust yourself to bounce back. If you skip a planned workout for a few days, you can still restart. This flexible mindset treats slip-ups as detours, not dead ends.

11.3 Positive Visualization
Occasionally, imagine yourself handling tasks calmly and efficiently. This mental rehearsal can prime your brain for success. It might feel

odd, but picturing yourself succeeding can lower anxiety and boost a sense of capability.

12. Everyday Confidence Boosters

- **Post-It Affirmations**: Short messages like "I'm resourceful" or "I handle challenges one step at a time" placed around your space can subtly shift your mindset.
- **Morning Routines**: Start the day with a small accomplishment—like making your bed or writing a quick to-do list. This sets a confident tone before other responsibilities arise.

13. When Self-Esteem Issues Become Overwhelming

13.1 Signs It Is Serious
If you constantly feel worthless, hopeless, or avoid interactions because you believe you have nothing to offer, you might be dealing with deeper self-esteem challenges that require professional help.

13.2 Possible Co-Existing Conditions
Women with ADHD sometimes also face anxiety or depression, which can further damage self-confidence. A trained counselor or psychiatrist can assess whether medication or specialized therapy is needed.

13.3 Emergency Assistance
If thoughts of self-harm or severe despair arise, reach out immediately to a mental health hotline or emergency service. You do not have to handle extreme feelings alone. Talking to someone confidentially can provide immediate relief and next steps.

14. Long-Term Outlook

14.1 Gradual Growth
Confidence does not arrive in one day. It unfolds slowly, with each strategy, each success, and each learning from failure. Expect ups and downs, but also trust that consistent effort creates lasting change.

14.2 Rewriting Your Story
By carefully questioning negative beliefs, setting healthy goals, and surrounding yourself with supportive influences, you begin telling yourself a new story—one where ADHD is part of who you are but not the sum total of your identity, and where your worth is built on more than any single mistake.

Chapter 15: Personal Growth and Emotional Well-Being

Personal growth is about exploring new ways to understand yourself and adapt to changes in life. Emotional well-being is tied to how you handle stress, cope with sadness, and find moments of peace or contentment. When a woman has ADHD, the process of personal growth and maintaining emotional stability can feel more complicated. You might have strong ups and downs, get sidetracked by distractions, or feel uncertainty about your long-term goals. Yet, there are paths to growing as a person while also caring for your emotional health in a way that fits an ADHD mind. Below, we will look at approaches and ideas you can try to help expand your sense of self, keep your moods balanced, and feel more at home in your own mind.

---

1. Understanding Personal Growth with ADHD

Personal growth often involves choosing an area of life to improve. This might be building stronger relationships, developing patience, or refining skills. For women with ADHD, there can be internal barriers:

1. **Overwhelm**: You might have so many ideas and plans that it is hard to pick just one to focus on.
2. **Inconsistent Motivation**: You might feel very driven one day and struggle to do anything the next.
3. **Imposter Feelings**: Past failures or forgetfulness can cause you to doubt your abilities.

These challenges do not mean you cannot grow. They simply mean you may need more deliberate strategies. Keep in mind that growth does not have to be fast. Even small, steady steps can lead to meaningful changes over time.

---

2. Exploring Your Values

A valuable starting point for personal growth is clarifying what matters to you. If you are unsure where to direct your efforts, consider looking at core values.

- **Reflect on Past High Points**: Think about times you felt proud, content, or excited. What was happening? Were you working on a creative project, helping someone, or learning a new skill?
- **Identify Motivators**: Make a short list of things that energize you. Perhaps you love supporting friends, expressing yourself through art, or learning about science.
- **Notice Tensions**: Are there actions in your life that conflict with your ideals? For example, if you value kindness but find yourself snapping at loved ones when stressed, that mismatch might be an area to address.

By understanding what you care about most, you can direct your personal growth toward actions that align with those values. This alignment helps you remain motivated, even when ADHD symptoms appear.

---

3. Goal-Setting for Growth

Clear goals give structure to personal development. However, women with ADHD can be prone to setting overly large or vague goals. When the mind is full of possibilities, it is tempting to aim for big changes all at once. That can backfire and lead to quitting early.

3.1 Start with Small, Specific Goals

- Instead of "I want to be more patient," define a narrower goal: "I will count to five before responding when I feel angry."
- Instead of "I want to get healthy," you could choose: "I will walk for 20 minutes on Monday, Wednesday, and Friday."

3.2 Break Goals into Steps

- Write down the exact steps needed. For example, if your goal is to have more calm evenings, your steps might include turning off screens by 9 p.m., lighting a soft lamp, and reading a relaxing book for 20 minutes.
- If you want to improve a skill (like drawing), break it into small daily practices: "Sketch for 10 minutes each morning."

3.3 Track and Adjust

- Keep a simple record of whether you did your planned tasks. This can be a notebook, a phone app, or a wall calendar with check marks.
- If you skip a step, ask why. Were you too tired, did you forget, or did you lose interest? Adjust your plan to make it simpler or more interesting next time.

Goals that are small and realistic are more likely to be completed, giving you a sense of success that feeds further growth.

---

4. Emotional Well-Being: Key Elements

Your emotional well-being is influenced by many factors: the quality of your relationships, how much rest you get, and how you handle conflicts or stress. When you have ADHD, you may experience emotions with extra intensity. One minute you might be excited, and the next you might feel drained. Recognizing these shifts and having methods to smooth them out can protect your mental balance.

4.1 Emotional Awareness

- Practice pausing now and then to check in with yourself. Ask, "What am I feeling right now?" You might find that you are tense or worried without realizing it.
- Labeling emotions ("I feel sad," "I feel nervous," "I feel overwhelmed") can help you decide what action to take.

4.2 Self-Soothing Strategies

- Gentle breathing exercises: Breathe in for four counts, hold for a moment, then breathe out for four counts, repeating for a minute or two.
- Listening to calm music or using a soft blanket can ground you when your thoughts are racing.
- Taking a brief walk or stepping outside for fresh air can reset your mood.

4.3 Balanced Routines

- Consistent sleep times, regular meals, and short breaks throughout the day support mood stability.
- Over-commitment often leads to burnout. Learn to say no when your schedule is already full.

Maintaining emotional well-being is not about never feeling upset or down. Rather, it is about responding to those feelings in gentle, constructive ways.

---

5. Dealing with Emotional Swings

Many women with ADHD feel emotions quickly and strongly. These emotional waves can lead to impulsive decisions or big disagreements if not managed carefully. Below are suggestions for dealing with these intense fluctuations:

5.1 Identify Early Signs

- Notice physical changes: a faster heartbeat, tightness in your chest, or shaky hands.
- Spot negative thoughts: "This is hopeless," "They do not respect me," etc.

Recognizing these early clues allows you to pause before the emotion peaks.

5.2 Create a Pause Button

- Remove yourself briefly from the triggering situation. Even a 30-second pause can help you think more clearly.
- Use mental reminders: "I can handle this," or "I don't need to respond instantly."

5.3 Regroup After an Outburst

- If you did lash out at someone, apologize without dwelling on shame. State simply: "I'm sorry for my reaction. I got overwhelmed."

- Reflect on how you can handle a similar moment better next time. Maybe you need a scripted approach: "I'll step out of the room if I feel anger rising."

Emotional swings are not a personal failure. They are part of how many ADHD minds operate. With awareness, you can reduce the damage they may cause and gradually develop more consistent reactions.

---

6. Building Self-Reflection Habits

Self-reflection is checking in on your thoughts, actions, and feelings. It is crucial for ongoing personal development, especially if ADHD makes life feel scattered. Here are ways to build a habit of reflecting:

- **Daily or Weekly Reviews**: Spend a few minutes each evening or at the end of the week asking, "What went well?" and "What was tough?"
- **Journaling**: Write a short entry, focusing on specific events and your reactions. If writing is hard, try bullet points or voice memos.
- **Prompted Questions**: Use simple prompts like "Today, I learned…" or "One thing I'm grateful for is…" to guide your thoughts.

Regular self-reflection helps you see patterns. For example, you might notice you always feel more anxious after skipping breakfast or that you are more productive when you start tasks before noon. This insight guides better choices.

7. Finding Meaning in Challenges

Hardships can provide a chance to develop resilience. This does not mean welcoming negative experiences but acknowledging that struggles can highlight personal strengths and new perspectives. If you are facing a tough season—like job loss, health problems, or relationship issues—consider how it might guide you toward growth:

- **Learning Skills**: A conflict at work might teach you how to communicate more calmly.
- **Refining Priorities**: A health scare could push you to reexamine your daily habits and find gentler routines.
- **Expanding Empathy**: Going through a hard time can help you connect better with others who face similar struggles.

By viewing challenges as potential lessons, you minimize self-blame and open the door to more growth, even in difficult periods.

---

8. Creative Approaches to Personal Growth

Women with ADHD may thrive when personal development involves creative or hands-on methods. Traditional methods like reading self-help books might not always resonate. Some alternatives include:

- **Art or Music Activities**: Painting, sketching, or crafting can help you process emotions and explore new facets of yourself.
- **Movement-Based Ideas**: Mindful walking, gentle yoga, or dancing can raise self-awareness. You might notice how your body feels when you step carefully or coordinate with music.

- **Group Workshops**: Some libraries or community centers host workshops that blend personal development with a hands-on activity. This structure can keep your ADHD mind engaged.

These outlets give you a chance to explore new angles of growth without sitting still for long stretches or dealing with too much abstract information at once.

---

9. Emotional Boundaries with Others

Emotional well-being also depends on your connections. If you let other people's moods or criticisms control your feelings, you risk constant upset. Setting emotional boundaries can help:

- **Know Where You End and Others Begin**: Your friend or family member might be upset, but you do not have to absorb their frustration as your own.
- **Speak Up When Overloaded**: If a conversation is too heated, politely say, "I need to pause this topic. Let's return to it later."
- **Recognize Your Limits**: Sometimes, supporting a loved one's crisis can be draining. It is okay to say, "I'm sorry you're going through this, but I'm feeling overwhelmed. Can we find someone else to help too?"

By respecting your own mental space, you preserve energy for personal growth rather than being pulled into unnecessary drama.

---

10. Social Growth as Part of Personal Growth

We often think of personal growth as individual change, but healthy social connections can boost emotional health. They can also challenge you to expand your viewpoint. For instance:

- **Joining a Group**: Trying a local club or online forum that focuses on an interest you have can spark new passions. It also teaches cooperation and empathy.
- **Volunteering**: Helping others can add meaning to your life. It also puts your own issues in perspective.
- **Supportive Friendships**: Friends who root for you encourage your personal growth, while you also support them in their own paths. That mutual support can reduce isolation.

Balancing your personal reflection with shared experiences can create a fuller, richer environment in which to develop.

---

11. Seeking Professional Guidance

Sometimes, growth and emotional well-being can stall if deeper issues remain unaddressed. A therapist, counselor, or coach familiar with ADHD can be extremely helpful.

- **Therapy**: Whether it is individual therapy or group sessions, a trained professional can give tools to handle anxiety, depression, or low self-worth.
- **Coaching**: ADHD coaches specialize in organization, motivation, and daily management. They can help you set and reach goals step by step.
- **Support Groups**: Some groups are led by professionals, while others are peer-run. They offer a chance to share stories, gain tips, and feel less alone in your struggles.

Professional input can clarify hidden obstacles and open up fresh pathways for growth.

12. Spiritual or Inner Reflection

For some, personal growth includes exploring spirituality or reflecting on bigger questions about life. This does not have to mean formal religion—it can be anything that helps you connect with a sense of meaning beyond daily tasks.

- **Quiet Time**: A brief moment each day to consider what you are grateful for or to reflect on personal beliefs.
- **Meditation or Prayer**: Even short sessions can calm the ADHD mind and bring a sense of connectedness.
- **Reading Inspirational Writings**: Uplifting quotes or short passages can shift your mindset and help you see problems from a broader view.

Such practices can nurture a sense of inner calm and purpose, which supports emotional balance.

---

13. Keeping Momentum

One major issue for women with ADHD is starting strong but losing interest. Personal growth and emotional health need ongoing attention:

1. **Periodic Reviews**: At least once a month, look at your goals or emotional well-being. Ask, "Am I still working toward these goals? Do they need updating?"
2. **Flexible Approaches**: If a method becomes dull, adjust it. For example, if journaling feels stale, try voice recordings or a drawing-based approach.
3. **Rewards and Encouragement**: Treat yourself when you maintain a positive habit for a certain time. A small treat or

personal note saying, "I stuck with my evening walk for two weeks!" can motivate you to keep it up.

Momentum does not mean constant excitement. Rather, it is a steady pattern of small actions that accumulate over time.

---

14. Handling Plateaus and Setbacks

Expect to hit plateaus, where progress seems slow, or face setbacks that undo some of your gains. These are normal parts of growth. Suggestions for when progress stalls:

- **Revisit Your Motivation**: Remind yourself why you wanted to change in the first place. Reconnect with your core values or long-term hopes.
- **Talk with Someone**: A friend, coach, or therapist can help you see if you need a new angle or more patience.
- **Celebrate What You Did Manage**: Even if you did not meet the entire goal, you might have learned a useful skill or discovered what does not work for you. That insight can guide your next steps.

Chapter 16: Money Management

Money management can be a complicated area for many adults. When you add ADHD into the mix, you might face extra hurdles: impulsive shopping, difficulty tracking bills, forgetting payment dates, or feeling overwhelmed by budgeting. Yet, having ADHD does not mean you cannot handle finances effectively. It only means you need systems that play to your strengths and minimize the areas where you are most vulnerable. In this chapter, we will go through practical steps and suggestions for managing your money in a way that fits an ADHD mind, helping you feel more secure and in control.

---

1. Recognizing ADHD-Related Financial Challenges

1. **Impulsive Buying**: You might see something appealing and purchase it on a whim without thinking about future bills.
2. **Disorganization**: Piles of unopened statements or scattered receipts can lead to confusion about what is owed or how much money is left.
3. **Forgetting Due Dates**: If paying a bill slips your mind, you might face late fees or damage your credit score.
4. **Boredom with Routine Tasks**: Setting and sticking to a budget can feel dull, causing you to skip essential steps.

Acknowledging these challenges is not about labeling yourself as bad with money. It is about identifying the ADHD-related patterns so you can find fitting strategies.

---

2. Creating a Budget That Works for You

A budget is a plan for how you will use your money. Traditional budgeting can feel restrictive or complicated for someone with ADHD. But you can adapt budgeting so it becomes simpler and more intuitive.

2.1 Start with Basic Categories

List your core expenses and income:

- **Income**: Paychecks, freelance earnings, or other sources.
- **Fixed Expenses**: Rent, mortgage, utilities, insurance, car payments.
- **Variable Expenses**: Groceries, gas, household items, personal care.
- **Fun or Extras**: Dining out, hobbies, small treats.

2.2 Pick a Format You Like

- **Paper and Pen**: A simple notebook where you write down monthly income and expenses.
- **Spreadsheet**: Programs like Excel or Google Sheets can do calculations for you if you set them up.
- **Budget Apps**: Some apps link to bank accounts, automatically categorizing spending. Look for apps that have straightforward layouts.

2.3 Make It ADHD-Friendly

- Keep categories broad. Too much detail can overwhelm you.
- Use visuals or color coding if that helps you see your spending at a glance.
- Update it in short, frequent bursts—maybe 5 minutes every other day—rather than one long session each month.

By choosing a budgeting method that feels natural, you raise the chance you will stick with it.

---

3. Setting Up Automated Systems

If forgetting payment dates is an issue, automation can rescue you from late fees. Most banks and bill providers offer options to automatically transfer or charge your account on a set day each month.

- **Automatic Bill Pay**: Ensure your rent or mortgage, utilities, phone bill, and insurance are paid without manual effort.
- **Linked Accounts**: Some people set up a separate bank account just for bills, transferring a fixed amount of money each pay period into that account.
- **Credit Card Autopay**: You can automate at least the minimum payment on your credit card. This helps avoid missed payments. However, watch your balance to keep from overspending.

Automation reduces the mental load on your ADHD mind. You do not need to hold those payment dates in your memory if the system does it for you.

---

4. Handling Impulsive Spending

Impulsivity can put a big dent in finances. Whether it is online shopping at midnight or buying items you do not need, these urges can sabotage your budget. Suggestions:

4.1 Delay the Purchase

- Give yourself a rule: wait 24 hours before buying anything above a set dollar amount (e.g., $50 or $100). This can let the initial urge pass if the item is not truly important.

4.2 Block Easy Spending

- Remove stored credit card info from online shopping sites. If you have to get up and physically find your card, you have more time to reconsider.
- Use a separate, low-limit credit card for everyday expenses so you cannot overspend beyond that limit.

4.3 Budget for Treats

- If you enjoy occasional "fun spending," build it into your plan. For example, give yourself a small monthly amount for impulsive buys. Once that amount is used up, you stop until next month.
- This approach acknowledges that some spontaneous treats can be okay if they are already accounted for in your budget.

---

5. Simplifying Bills and Accounts

Multiple bank accounts, credit cards, and subscription services can overwhelm an ADHD mind. Try to simplify:

1. **Fewer Credit Cards**: Having too many increases the risk of forgetting a bill or misunderstanding your debt.
2. **Consolidate Debt**: If you have various small debts, see if you can combine them into one loan with a lower interest rate. This makes payments more straightforward.

3. **List Subscriptions**: Services like streaming platforms or monthly boxes can quietly eat away at your budget. Cancel those you rarely use.

Simplicity helps you keep track without feeling buried in details.

6. Tracking Spending Without Boredom

Traditional money tracking can be dull. Here are ways to make it more engaging:

- **Color-Coded Charts**: Use highlighters or digital color coding to mark spending categories in a calendar.
- **Frequent Short Check-Ins**: Instead of one big monthly check, do quick daily or weekly reviews. This can be less overwhelming and more ADHD-friendly.
- **Spending Challenges**: Some people use a fun approach, like a "no-spend day" each week or trying to spend under a certain limit at the grocery store. Turn it into a game.

Anything that brings a little fun or immediate feedback can help an ADHD mind stay with the task.

7. Saving Strategies

Saving can feel abstract, especially if ADHD makes you live more in the present moment. Yet, having savings lessens stress when sudden expenses appear.

7.1 Pay Yourself First

- Right when you receive income, set aside a small percentage into a savings account—before you pay bills or buy anything else. This way, you do not "forget" to save.

7.2 Use a Separate Bank

- If possible, put savings into a bank that is not your main checking account. The extra step of transferring money back can reduce impulsive withdrawals.

7.3 Set Goals

- Saving is easier with a clear purpose. Maybe you want an emergency fund of one month's expenses, or you want to buy a car eventually. Label your savings account with the goal's name to keep it real in your mind.

Even small amounts saved regularly can build up over time. Consistency matters more than the size of each deposit.

---

8. Getting Out of Debt

Debt can add stress, especially with ADHD. You might forget about balances, making the situation worse. To manage debt more effectively:

8.1 Understand Your Total Debt

- Collect all statements or log in to each account. Make a list of the debts, their balances, and their interest rates. Yes, it can be uncomfortable, but it is crucial to see the whole picture.

8.2 Prioritize Payments

- Some prefer the "debt snowball" approach: pay extra toward the smallest debt first for a quick win. Others use the "debt avalanche" method: pay extra on the highest-interest debt first to save on fees.
- Pick whichever method feels more motivating. The important thing is to be consistent.

8.3 Automate When Possible

- Set up automatic extra payments toward your chosen debt. This helps you avoid forgetting or being tempted to spend that money elsewhere.

Clearing debts step by step builds financial confidence, especially if ADHD has led to long-standing money worries.

---

9. Partner and Family Finances

If you share finances with a partner or spouse, ADHD can influence how you handle money together. You might resent a partner's spending or feel guilty if you are the one overspending. To reduce tension:

- **Open Communication**: Talk openly about challenges. Explain that ADHD can lead to impulsivity or disorganization, not that you do not care about finances.
- **Split Responsibilities**: If your partner is more organized with bills, maybe they handle that part while you focus on grocery shopping or financial research. Use each person's strengths.
- **Joint Planning**: Have a monthly meeting to check on shared goals, review bills, and adapt the plan if needed. Keep the meeting short and focused.

Approaching money as a team prevents blame and helps you both see progress together.

---

10. Handling Paperwork and Receipts

Paper clutter can build up, making it difficult to track spending or find important documents. Ideas:

1. **Designate a Drop Zone**: Keep one spot (a tray or folder) where you put all incoming receipts or bills. This way, they are not scattered around the house.
2. **Schedule a Weekly Paper Sort**: Sort the tray's contents into categories: "To Pay," "To File," or "To Recycle."
3. **Go Digital if Possible**: Switch to electronic statements to reduce paper. Be sure to create an organized folder on your computer or cloud storage for these files.

Routine and simple systems cut down on chaos.

---

11. Self-Control Tools

Imposing external checks on your ADHD impulses can help:

- **Use Cash**: When you shop with cash, you have a physical limit. Once the cash is gone, you cannot buy more. This is a tangible way to see your spending in real-time.
- **Buddy Accountability**: Ask a trusted friend or family member to review your finances once a month. Knowing someone else will see your spending might discourage impulse buys.
- **Lock Up Cards**: For truly extreme impulse issues, consider keeping credit cards in a safe place at home so you cannot use them spontaneously when you are out.

A little friction can slow you down enough to make wiser choices.

---

12. Planning for Big Expenses

Larger expenses, like vacations, new furniture, or special events, require forward planning. For someone with ADHD, it is easy to jump into big spending without thorough preparation. Steps:

1. **Research**: Gather prices and estimates. Make a rough plan of how much you need to save.
2. **Timeline**: Decide when you want this expense. Work backward to see how much money you need to set aside each month or week.
3. **Keep Reminders**: Put a note or a picture of the item or destination on your fridge or in your planner. This keeps the goal visible and helps you resist random spending that could derail your plan.

Thinking ahead is not always natural with ADHD, but using visual cues and simple breakdowns can make it more approachable.

---

13. Emotional Side of Money

Money is not just numbers. It ties to emotions like security, fear, or shame—especially if ADHD mishaps have led to family conflicts or personal stress. Suggestions for managing the emotional aspect:

- **Forgive Past Mistakes**: You might feel guilty about debts or missed opportunities. Guilt alone will not fix things. Focus on what you can do now.

- **Self-Reward**: Recognize small improvements. If you stayed on budget this week, perhaps watch a free movie at home or treat yourself to a nice snack within reason.
- **Seek Therapy**: If financial issues cause severe anxiety or argue with family members, a counselor can help untangle those feelings.

When you handle the emotional layers, it becomes easier to stick to your money plan and gain confidence in your ability to manage it.

---

14. Building Credit Wisely

For many large goals—like buying a house or car—credit scores matter. A low credit score can mean higher interest rates. Women with ADHD may harm their credit score through late payments or maxed-out cards. Steps to improve credit:

1. **Pay On Time**: Even if it is just the minimum payment, do it before the deadline. Automation helps a lot here.
2. **Keep Balances Low**: Use only a portion of your available credit. Maxing out a card signals risk to lenders.
3. **Check Reports**: Get a free copy of your credit report annually. Look for errors or signs of fraud. If you spot mistakes, dispute them.

Responsible credit use takes practice but is key to better financial opportunities later on.

---

15. Investing Basics

Once you have your budget stable and some savings built, you might think about investing. This might be in a retirement plan at work, mutual funds, or other options. For an ADHD-friendly approach:

- **Simplify**: If your workplace offers a retirement plan, start with a small percentage of your pay. Increase it gradually. Choose a straightforward fund if you are not comfortable picking individual stocks.
- **Automate**: Have contributions taken from your paycheck or bank account automatically. This way, you do not have to remember to invest each time.
- **Learn Gradually**: If investing interests you, learn in small steps—perhaps watch short educational videos or read simple guides about basic investing ideas.

Keep it simple to avoid confusion or overwhelm.

---

16. When to Seek Professional Help

If money issues are severe—constant overdrafts, large unpaid debts, or frequent conflicts—it might be time to talk with a professional:

- **Financial Advisor**: They can help you set goals, create a workable budget, and guide you on saving or investing. Look for someone who is patient and respects that ADHD might require unique tactics.
- **Credit Counselor**: Non-profit credit counseling agencies offer advice on managing debt or negotiating with creditors. They can also help you set up a debt repayment plan.
- **Therapist**: If money problems tie into deeper emotional struggles, a counselor can support you in breaking patterns of self-sabotage or impulsive behavior.

Admitting you need help is a smart move, not a sign of failure. A trained professional can save you time, stress, and further financial trouble.

17. Tracking Progress and Staying Motivated

Money management is an ongoing process. You might do well for a month, then slip back into old habits. ADHD can increase those slip-ups. To stay on course:

1. **Monthly Money Check**: Schedule a quick session (15–30 minutes) at the same time each month to go over your finances. Mark it in your calendar so you will not forget.
2. **Reward Positive Outcomes**: Each time you pay down a chunk of debt or stay on budget for a month, recognize it. That small nudge of pride can keep you going.
3. **Revise as Needed**: If a system stops working—maybe the app you used is too cluttered—try a new approach. Flexibility is key.

It is normal to have setbacks. The goal is not perfect discipline, but steadily improving money habits that adapt to your ADHD nature.

18. Building a Future You Want

Money is a tool. Used well, it can open doors to experiences, security, and less daily worry. For women with ADHD, the journey to feeling comfortable with finances can be bumpy, but each step forward—like automating bills, limiting impulsive buys, or growing a small savings account—builds a stronger foundation. Over time, you can go from feeling anxious about money to feeling more relaxed and even excited about what you can achieve.

Chapter 17: Mindfulness Practices

Mindfulness is often described as paying attention on purpose. It involves noticing what is happening in the present without judging it. For many women with ADHD, the idea of quietly focusing on one thing seems challenging. The mind can bounce from one thought to another, and it can be hard to stay still. Yet, mindfulness practices can help reduce stress, sharpen focus, and bring more calm into everyday life. They do not require changing who you are; rather, they offer tools that support a calmer and clearer state of mind—something especially useful when ADHD makes life feel scattered.

Below, we will look at different methods to practice mindfulness in a way that suits an active or easily distracted mind. We will also cover how mindfulness can fit into daily routines, how it can help with emotional ups and downs, and how to adapt practices so they feel doable rather than overwhelming.

---

1. Understanding Mindfulness in Simple Terms

Many people think mindfulness means sitting cross-legged and emptying the mind of all thoughts. But that image can feel unrealistic. In reality, mindfulness is about being aware of your inner and outer world in a clear, gentle way. Here are some basics:

- **Present-Moment Attention**: Instead of worrying about the future or rehashing the past, mindfulness encourages you to notice what is happening right now—such as how your breath feels or what you see around you.
- **Non-Judgment**: When thoughts or emotions appear, you do not label them as good or bad. You simply recognize them:

"There is a worried thought," or "I am feeling impatient right now."
- **Gentleness**: If your attention wanders, you calmly bring it back, again and again, without scolding yourself.

For women with ADHD, this approach can take practice. It might be tempting to say, "I cannot sit still, so mindfulness is not for me." But there are many forms of mindfulness that involve movement, brief sessions, or creative outlets.

---

2. Benefits of Mindfulness for ADHD

Mindfulness can help reduce restlessness, impulsivity, and negative self-talk. It can also ease stress by offering a pause before reacting to things. Some specific benefits include:

1. **Improved Focus**: By training yourself to return your mind to the present moment, you build skills that might help with tasks like reading, writing, or listening in meetings.
2. **Better Emotional Regulation**: Mindfulness encourages noticing emotions early. You might spot frustration rising before it becomes an outburst.
3. **Lower Anxiety**: Focusing on right now can lessen worries about tomorrow or guilt about yesterday.
4. **Kinder Self-Image**: When you practice non-judgment, you learn to be less critical of every slip or flaw. This can boost self-esteem over time.
5. **Less Reactivity**: Mindfulness introduces a brief pause between an event and your response, which is especially helpful if you tend to act impulsively.

These changes do not show up overnight, but consistent practice—even in small doses—can bring real improvements.

3. Short, Simple Exercises

Starting small is key. If you try to meditate for 30 minutes right away, ADHD restlessness might take over. Instead, try brief exercises:

3.1 One-Minute Breathing

- Sit or stand comfortably.
- Close your eyes if you want, or let them rest on a neutral spot.
- Breathe in, noticing the air filling your lungs, and breathe out, noticing the release.
- Keep your mind on the sensation of breathing. If thoughts wander, gently return focus to the breath.
- After a minute, stop.

This is a tiny practice, but doing it daily can introduce you to the calm feeling of mindful attention.

3.2 Five Senses Check

- Pause and name five things you can see (a lamp, a painting, the sky, your shoes, your hands).
- Next, name four things you can touch (the chair, your shirt, a pen, your hair).
- Then, three things you can hear (birds, traffic, an air conditioner).
- Two things you can smell (maybe food, perfume, or fresh air).
- One thing you can taste (gum, toothpaste, coffee).

This simple method anchors you in the present by tapping into your senses, cutting through racing thoughts.

3.3 Mindful Moments

- Choose an everyday task: washing hands, walking to the mailbox, or sipping tea.
- Focus solely on that activity. Notice the temperature of the water, the feel of the ground under your feet, or the flavor of the drink.
- Any time your mind drifts, bring it back to the immediate sensations.

Even a 20-second mindful moment can help you see how often the mind wanders and practice bringing it back.

---

4. Movement-Based Mindfulness

If sitting still feels impossible, you can try mindfulness that incorporates movement:

4.1 Mindful Walking

- Walk at a relaxed pace, paying attention to each step.
- Notice how your foot lifts, moves, and touches the ground.
- Observe the rhythm of your breath as you walk.
- When you realize you are thinking of something else, gently refocus on the movement and surroundings.

4.2 Stretching

- Stand up, do a slow stretch, and pay attention to how your muscles feel.
- Notice areas of tightness or release.
- Breathe deeply as you hold each stretch, letting the breath guide your movement.

4.3 Yoga or Tai Chi

- These structured practices blend physical poses or movements with breath awareness.
- Even a brief session (five to ten minutes) can build mindfulness if you focus on each movement and sensation.
- Look for beginner-friendly videos or local classes that emphasize slow, mindful transitions rather than fast-paced exercise.

Movement-based mindfulness can be ideal for ADHD because it gives your body something to do, making it easier to remain present.

---

5. Adapting Mindfulness to an ADHD Mind

Traditional mindfulness instructions sometimes say, "Sit silently for 30 minutes, watching your thoughts." This can be too big a leap for someone whose mind races or whose body craves movement. Consider these adaptations:

- **Short Sessions**: Two-minute or five-minute blocks done throughout the day may work better than one long session.
- **Use Timers**: A gentle timer can remind you when to start and stop, reducing the urge to watch the clock.
- **Allow Fidgets**: Holding a stress ball or small smooth stone while you focus on the breath can help channel restlessness.
- **Focus on Sensory Inputs**: If breath awareness bores you, consider listening to calming sounds or focusing on a candle flame.
- **Guided Recordings**: Listening to a guided session can provide structure. Many mindfulness apps offer short practices of varying lengths.

The key is flexibility. There is no single "correct" way to practice mindfulness, especially for a mind that naturally bounces around.

---

6. Handling the Wandering Mind

Your mind will wander. That is normal. The wandering is not failure; the moment you notice it and gently return to the present is the real practice. Think of it as mental push-ups: each time you catch yourself lost in thought and bring yourself back, you strengthen the "attention muscle."

- **No Self-Blame**: If your mind drifts 50 times in a short session, that is 50 chances to practice returning.
- **Label Thoughts**: When you notice you are thinking about dinner, just label it "planning thought" or "hungry thought," then refocus on your breath or your environment.
- **Pat Yourself on the Back**: Acknowledge each successful moment of awareness. "I caught myself drifting—good job noticing!"

Over time, noticing the wandering sooner can improve. But even with regular practice, the mind still wanders. That is the human condition, not just ADHD.

---

7. Mindfulness for Emotional Regulation

Women with ADHD may have powerful emotional surges—feeling very excited, frustrated, or sad in a short time. Mindfulness helps by giving a method to step back from intense feelings and see them as passing events rather than permanent truths.

7.1 Observing Emotions

- When a strong emotion arises, pause to identify it: "I feel anger," or "I feel fear."
- Notice its effect on your body: clenched fists, rapid heartbeat, tense shoulders.
- Let the emotion exist without trying to push it away or cling to it. Watch how it shifts over time.

7.2 Breathing Through Emotions

- When overwhelmed, focus on slow, deep breaths. This can calm the body's stress response.
- With each exhale, imagine releasing a bit of the tension or worry.

7.3 Writing It Out

- If sitting quietly is too hard when upset, try a "mindful journaling" moment. Write your feelings for a few minutes in short, direct words: "I am angry because..." This can transform jumbled emotions into clearer language.

Mindfulness does not erase emotions but can prevent them from running your life by offering a space between feeling and reacting.

---

8. Incorporating Mindfulness into Daily Routines

One big hurdle is remembering to be mindful when busy or stressed. By weaving mindfulness into daily tasks, you form habits:

- **Morning Mindful Pause**: Before leaving bed, take five slow breaths, noticing your body and the day's first sensations.

- **Mindful Meals**: At least once a day, eat a meal or snack without scrolling on your phone. Pay attention to flavors, textures, and the act of chewing.
- **Transition Times**: When moving from one task to another—like finishing work and starting dinner—pause for a few calm breaths to shift gears.
- **Evening Wind-Down**: Try a short relaxation method—breathing, gentle stretching, or scanning your body for tension—before sleeping.

Making mindfulness part of established routines helps you avoid feeling like you have to create extra time for it.

---

9. Technology and Apps

Many mindfulness apps exist. While ADHD can cause you to lose interest in an app over time, the right one can help keep sessions short and engaging:

- **Guided Meditations**: Apps provide brief, spoken instructions that walk you through focusing on breath, sensations, or calming imagery.
- **Progress Tracking**: Some apps let you log each session, offering simple streaks or stats that might motivate you.
- **Reminders**: You can set notifications to prompt a quick mindful break. But be mindful of too many alerts, which might become noise.
- **Selectable Durations**: If one day you only have two minutes, choose a short practice. If another day you feel calm, try a 10-minute session.

Choose an app with a friendly tone and variety, so you can switch techniques when you get bored.

10. Mindful Self-Compassion

Women with ADHD can carry guilt about mistakes or focus on perceived flaws. Mindful self-compassion adds kindness into the practice:

- **Acknowledge Struggle**: When you feel down about forgetting a task or acting impulsively, gently name the pain: "This is tough right now."
- **Remind Yourself You Are Human**: Understand that everyone messes up sometimes. ADHD might magnify certain errors, but imperfection is part of life for all people.
- **Place a Hand Over Your Heart**: This small gesture can feel soothing, as if you are sending warmth to yourself.
- **Offer Kind Words**: Silently say, "It is okay to make mistakes. I am learning. I can handle this with time."

Self-compassion does not excuse poor behavior; it provides a supportive base for making changes without beating yourself up.

---

11. Mindful Listening and Communication

In relationships or group settings, ADHD might cause you to interrupt or lose track of what others say. Mindful listening involves:

1. **Concentrated Attention**: When someone speaks, aim to keep your mind on their words. Watch their expression and tone.
2. **Pause Before Replying**: Let their words sink in. Count one or two seconds after they stop speaking to see if they have more to say.
3. **Reflect**: Paraphrase what you heard: "So you are saying you feel overlooked at work?" This shows you are paying attention.

4. **Stay Curious**: If your mind wanders, bring it back with a question: "Can you tell me more about that?"

This skill can reduce misunderstandings and help you connect better with friends, family, or coworkers.

---

12. Group Mindfulness or Classes

If practicing alone feels challenging, consider a group setting:

- **Community Sessions**: Some community centers or health clinics host guided mindfulness classes. A group atmosphere can bring structure.
- **ADHD-Focused Programs**: Look for coaches or counselors who specialize in ADHD and mindfulness, blending practical tips with mindful training.
- **Online Groups**: Virtual sessions can let you practice with others from the comfort of home.

A supportive environment can keep you on track, answer your questions, and help you feel less alone in your struggles.

---

13. Overcoming Common Obstacles

13.1 "I Don't Have Time"

- Try micro-sessions: even 30 seconds to tune in to your breath can make a difference.
- Pair mindfulness with something you already do, such as brushing your teeth or waiting for coffee to brew.

13.2 "My Mind Just Won't Stop Racing"

- Racing thoughts are normal. The goal is not to force them away but to see them clearly and gently redirect attention.
- Movement-based or guided mindfulness may work better than sitting in silence.

13.3 "I'm Too Impatient"

- View impatience itself as a topic of mindfulness. Notice the feeling of wanting to speed up or finish.
- Start very small—just a minute. If that feels too long, do half a minute. The key is to build a habit gradually.

13.4 "I Tried It Once and It Didn't Work"

- Mindfulness is like learning any skill. One session might not spark immediate calm or focus. Consistency is key, and results usually show over weeks or months of short, regular practice.

---

14. Integrating Mindfulness with Other Strategies

Mindfulness is not a stand-alone cure for ADHD. It works best alongside other strategies:

- **Medication**: If you use ADHD medication, mindfulness might further improve attention by helping you manage internal distractions.
- **Therapy or Coaching**: You can talk with a professional about emotional blocks that mindfulness reveals. They can offer personalized guidance.
- **Organizational Tools**: A mindful approach to using calendars or to-do lists can reduce the chance you will ignore them.

- **Healthy Lifestyle**: Good sleep, balanced nutrition, and physical activity all support a clearer mind, making mindfulness easier to maintain.

Seeing mindfulness as part of a bigger toolkit ensures you get the most benefit from each element.

---

15. Measuring Progress

Mindfulness improvements are often subtle. You might notice:

1. **Slightly Less Reactivity**: Perhaps you pause more before responding in tense conversations.
2. **Moments of Clarity**: You catch yourself lost in daydreams and refocus more quickly than before.
3. **Reduced Stress**: Daily hassles might not trigger as much anxiety or anger.
4. **Better Self-Kindness**: Instead of harsh self-criticism, you find more patient and understanding thoughts.

No one becomes 100% calm or perfectly attentive. Small shifts, repeated over time, can add up to a more balanced way of living.

---

16. Addressing Misconceptions

16.1 "Mindfulness Is Religious"
While mindfulness has roots in certain spiritual traditions, modern approaches often focus on practical mental health benefits. You can practice it in a purely secular way, treating it as a mental exercise.

16.2 "I Must Empty My Mind"
It is basically impossible to have zero thoughts. The practice is to notice and gently manage thoughts, not eradicate them.

16.3 "I Have to Be Perfect at It"

There is no pass or fail. The "success" is in noticing when you drift off and calmly returning your attention.

---

17. Encouraging Others Around You

If you live with family or friends, inviting them to practice mindfulness with you can offer support:

- **Shared Quiet Time**: Spend a few minutes in silence together after dinner or before bed.
- **Mindful Family Moments**: During a meal, ask everyone to focus on the taste and texture of the first bite.
- **Respect Boundaries**: Not everyone will be interested, and that is okay. Leading by example might quietly influence them later.

Having a partner or friend who also practices mindfulness can help keep you motivated and provide an outlet to share experiences.

---

18. Mindfulness at Work or School

Mindfulness can help you stay organized and calm in professional or academic settings. Some options:

- **Micro-Breaks**: Every hour, take 30 seconds to breathe or stretch mindfully.
- **Mindful Email Checking**: Before opening your inbox, pause and take a breath to prepare for whatever you may see.
- **Scheduled Reminders**: Set a gentle phone alert at lunchtime for a 1-minute mindfulness break.

- **Avoid Multitasking**: As best you can, do one task at a time with full attention, then move on. This single-task approach is a form of mindfulness.

By weaving these habits into your work or study routine, you lower stress and might see improved performance over time.

---

19. What If Mindfulness Triggers Anxiety?

Sometimes, turning inward can stir anxious thoughts, especially if a person has unresolved emotional issues. If that happens:

- **Try External Focus**: Instead of focusing on breath or internal sensations, focus on sounds around you, an object in front of you, or slow walking.
- **Shorten the Practice**: Do 15 seconds at a time, gradually increasing if it feels okay.
- **Seek Professional Help**: A therapist can guide you through safe mindfulness techniques if anxiety is intense. They may suggest other coping strategies first.

Mindfulness should not feel like a mental battle. Adjust the approach to maintain a sense of safety.

Chapter 18: Hobbies and Personal Interests

Finding and enjoying hobbies can be a source of happiness, creativity, and relaxation—especially for women with ADHD, who sometimes struggle with staying engaged in everyday tasks. Hobbies allow you to explore your interests in a more open-ended setting, free from many of the pressures that come with work or household responsibilities. They can also serve as outlets for restless energy, ways to build confidence, and opportunities to meet like-minded people.

In this chapter, we will look at the value of hobbies, how to pick pursuits that match your ADHD style, how to manage challenges like boredom or distraction, and how to keep hobbies fun rather than stressful. Whether you love artistic pursuits, sports, learning new skills, or collecting, there is a hobby out there that can spark excitement and offer a refreshing break from daily routines.

---

1. Why Hobbies Matter for Women with ADHD

1.1 Creative Outlets
ADHD brains often overflow with ideas. A hobby—like painting, writing, crafting, or DIY projects—can channel that creative flow in a positive direction.

1.2 Stress Relief
Hobbies let you step away from daily stress. Focusing on something enjoyable can ease tension and give your mind a rest from worries.

1.3 Self-Discovery
When trying a new hobby, you learn about your style, likes, and dislikes. You might realize you enjoy detail-oriented tasks if they are tied to an interest, even if detail work at the office bores you.

1.4 Building Confidence

If work or school tasks highlight your ADHD weaknesses, a hobby can showcase strengths. You might feel empowered to see yourself excel at crocheting, pottery, or running, boosting self-esteem.

1.5 Social Connection

Group hobbies—like a book club, sports team, or dance class—provide a chance to meet people who share similar interests, creating community and friendships.

---

2. Identifying Your Passions and Interests

Choosing a hobby can feel overwhelming if you have broad curiosity or if you have lost touch with what you really enjoy. A few ways to explore:

- **Recall Childhood Joys**: What did you love doing as a kid? Drawing, building puzzles, riding a bike? Maybe those interests still hold appeal in grown-up forms.
- **Notice Curiosities**: If you are always watching cooking shows or intrigued by astronomy news, try cooking classes or a beginner telescope.
- **Experiment**: Pick a few low-cost or accessible hobbies to sample. Spend a month exploring each one in short bursts. You will see which ones spark excitement.
- **Ask Friends**: Friends might have hobbies you have never considered, like birdwatching or calligraphy. Try joining them once to see if it clicks.

There is no shame in trying multiple hobbies before finding one that truly fits. ADHD minds often enjoy variety and experimentation.

3. Matching Hobbies to Your ADHD Style

3.1 High-Energy vs. Calm

- If you have lots of physical energy, a hobby like hiking, dancing, or a sports league can be satisfying.
- If you need a calming influence, hobbies like painting, knitting, or meditation-related crafts can ground you.

3.2 Structured vs. Free-Form

- Some people thrive with clear rules, like board games, martial arts, or puzzle-solving.
- Others prefer open creativity, such as writing stories, painting freely, or making music without strict guidelines.

3.3 Social vs. Solo

- Group hobbies like community theater or a choir let you interact and stay motivated by social ties.
- Solo hobbies, like gardening or reading, can offer peaceful alone time if social interaction drains you.

Try to match the hobby's structure and energy level to what feels most comfortable for your ADHD traits. Remember, you can also balance multiple hobbies if you have varied interests.

---

4. Starting a New Hobby Without Overdoing It

Many ADHD adults leap into a new pastime with huge excitement, buying all the gear or supplies. Then interest wanes, leaving behind clutter and guilt. To prevent that:

4.1 Start Small

- Borrow materials from a friend or library instead of buying everything.
- Do a free trial class if possible.
- Limit your initial supply investment until you are sure you want to continue.

4.2 Manage Excitement

- If you are brimming with enthusiasm, remind yourself that it is okay to grow gradually. You do not need the top-of-the-line camera on day one if trying photography.

4.3 Set a Trial Period

- Commit to exploring a hobby for a set time—maybe four weeks. During that time, track how you feel. If you still love it at the end, consider deeper involvement.

This approach reduces wasted money or space if the passion fizzles out quickly.

---

5. Maintaining Interest and Avoiding Boredom

ADHD minds can lose excitement once the novelty fades. Here are strategies to keep a hobby fresh:

5.1 Break It into Projects

- Instead of saying, "I'll write a novel," set smaller goals: "Outline one chapter this week," or "Write 500 words."
- Tangible milestones help you see progress and maintain motivation.

5.2 Vary Your Approach

- If you paint, try different subjects, mediums, or techniques.
- If you run, pick new routes or find a friendly 5K event.
- Keeping the challenge level and variety alive can spark renewed interest.

5.3 Set Social Accountability

- Join a club or online forum related to your hobby. Share updates, photos, or achievements.
- Knowing you will discuss progress with others can push you to keep going.

5.4 Shuffle Between Two or Three Hobbies

- If you have multiple interests, rotate among them rather than forcing yourself to stick to one until burnout.
- Just be sure not to spread yourself so thin that you never grow in any single skill.

---

6. Handling ADHD Hurdles in Hobbies

Even enjoyable activities can face ADHD-related obstacles:

6.1 Distracting Thoughts

- Keep a notepad nearby. If random to-dos or ideas pop up, jot them down quickly and return to the hobby. This prevents mental clutter from pulling you away.

6.2 Time Management

- If hyperfocus happens, you might lose track of time and neglect other tasks. Set a timer or alarm to remind yourself to pause or switch tasks.

6.3 Frustration with Mistakes

- Perfectionism can creep in. Reframe errors as part of the learning process, especially in creative or skill-based hobbies.

6.4 Overcommitting

- Be mindful not to sign up for too many workshops, clubs, or events at once. Keep your schedule realistic so your hobby remains a source of joy, not stress.

---

7. Turning Hobbies into Social Connections

Hobbies can open doors to friendships and a sense of belonging:

7.1 Local Groups

- Check community bulletin boards, library listings, or online platforms for clubs or groups that match your hobby.
- Attending regular meetings can help you stay consistent and meet potential friends.

7.2 Workshops and Classes

- Taking a class in pottery, baking, or a foreign language can be a fun way to learn while meeting classmates.
- Instructors can also offer structured feedback, helpful if ADHD causes you to miss certain details.

7.3 Online Communities

- From social media groups to specialized forums, you can share tips, ask questions, and show off your projects.
- This is especially handy if you live in an area where local communities for your interest are scarce.

Being around people who share your passion can motivate you and reduce feelings of isolation.

---

8. Balancing Hobbies with Responsibilities

Women with ADHD might get so immersed in a hobby that daily tasks (work deadlines, cleaning, or family time) are overlooked. A few suggestions:

1. **Schedule Playtime**: Plan specific windows for hobby activities. For example, "Two hours on Saturday afternoon are for painting." This can prevent guilt or conflict with other responsibilities.
2. **Use Hobbies as Rewards**: Tackle a dreaded chore or task, then enjoy a set period of your hobby as a "treat" for finishing the chore.
3. **Communicate with Family or Partners**: If you live with others, make sure they know your hobby time is important to you. Arrange fair distribution of tasks so you can focus guilt-free.
4. **Keep a Visible Calendar**: Mark in your hobby sessions. Seeing them in the same calendar as your to-do list or appointments helps you maintain balance.

Healthy boundaries ensure that hobbies stay enjoyable and do not become another stress point.

9. Low-Cost or Free Hobby Ideas

Hobbies do not have to be expensive. Some budget-friendly or free ideas:

- **Reading**: Libraries offer free book borrowing, and e-books or audio books can be borrowed online.
- **Nature Walks/Hiking**: Minimal equipment needed beyond comfortable shoes.
- **Journaling or Creative Writing**: Just pen and paper (or a computer) required.
- **Photography with a Phone**: Most phones have decent cameras. Explore composition, lighting, or simple editing apps.
- **Drawing or Doodling**: Basic pencils and paper are enough to start.
- **Free Online Tutorials**: Many platforms have free lessons on coding, crafting, or playing instruments.

Starting with something low-cost can reduce the pressure if you lose interest or switch to something else. You can always invest more later.

---

10. Tech-Related Hobbies

If you enjoy gadgets or staying online, certain tech hobbies might be appealing:

- **Digital Art**: Using drawing tablets or graphic design software can channel creativity.
- **Coding**: Learning basic programming can be mentally engaging. There are many free resources for beginners.
- **Video Editing or Podcasting**: If you like storytelling, you could produce short videos or audio content.
- **Online Games**: Cooperative games can foster teamwork and social interaction. Just keep an eye on time spent to avoid going down a rabbit hole.

For ADHD, ensure you set boundaries, so you do not hyperfocus for endless hours and neglect real-life needs.

---

11. Physical Hobbies for Restless Energy

Activities that incorporate movement can help release pent-up energy and support better focus afterward:

- **Dance Lessons**: Zumba, salsa, or hip-hop classes provide structured movement and fun music.
- **Team Sports**: Recreational leagues for soccer, volleyball, or softball can combine exercise and community.
- **Cycling**: Whether road biking or casual weekend rides, pedaling can clear the mind.
- **Rock Climbing**: This combines physical challenge with problem-solving.

Choose an intensity level that fits your fitness. If needed, start gently to avoid burnout or injury.

---

12. Hands-On Crafts and DIY

Many women with ADHD find satisfaction in tactile projects—using the hands and seeing tangible results:

- **Knitting or Crocheting**: Repetitive motions can be calming, and patterns offer structure.
- **Woodworking**: Basic DIY furniture or decorative items let you focus on precise tasks.
- **Home Projects**: Painting a room, decorating a space, or upcycling old furniture can tap creativity.

- **Jewelry Making**: Beading or wire wrapping can be a detailed process that engages concentration.

Plan ahead so you do not accumulate too many half-finished projects. Maybe set one main project at a time.

---

13. Collecting and Organizing

Collecting items—stamps, coins, vintage toys, or trading cards—can be exciting for ADHD minds that love new information or visuals. But watch for potential clutter. Systems to stay organized:

- **Clear Display**: Show items in labeled containers or on shelves, so you see them easily.
- **Rotate Focus**: If you collect multiple things, focus on one at a time to prevent chaos.
- **Budget Limits**: Make sure collecting does not turn into impulse buying that hurts your finances.

Collecting can be a hobby that merges curiosity, organization, and the thrill of finding rare pieces.

---

14. Turning Hobbies into Side Jobs—Pros and Cons

Some hobbies can become part-time businesses, like selling handmade crafts or offering photography services. This might look appealing if you love the hobby, but be cautious:

- **Pros**: Earning money from what you enjoy can be rewarding. It might motivate you to polish your skills.
- **Cons**: Turning fun into business adds pressure, deadlines, and client demands, which can zap the joy. ADHD might make business management tasks stressful.

- **Balance**: If you decide to do this, keep the scale manageable. Maybe start with small sales or commissions. If it feels too demanding, you can scale back to keep it purely for pleasure.

Think carefully before monetizing a hobby. Not every fun pursuit needs to become a revenue stream.

---

15. Hobbies for Relaxation and Mindfulness

As discussed in the previous chapter, hobbies can also double as mindfulness practice:

- **Coloring Books**: Adult coloring books can be soothing, focusing your mind on gentle repetitive strokes.
- **Gardening**: Tending plants involves sensory engagement—touching soil, watching growth—that can be therapeutic.
- **Puzzles**: Jigsaw puzzles or logic puzzles help you concentrate step by step.
- **Simple Music**: Playing an instrument casually can be meditative if you focus on the notes and rhythms.

These hobbies blend leisure with a mindful state, helping you unwind in a structured yet calming way.

---

16. Family and Group Hobbies

If you want to involve family or friends in your hobby time:

- **Family Game Night**: Board games, trivia, or puzzles can bring everyone together.
- **Cooking or Baking**: Testing recipes as a team fosters collaboration and skill-sharing.

- **Nature Outings**: Picnics, birdwatching, or short hiking trips can be educational and active.
- **Community Volunteering**: If you enjoy philanthropy, volunteering as a group can be a shared hobby that benefits others.

Shared hobbies can strengthen bonds and create enjoyable memories, but be mindful of each person's comfort level and attention span.

17. Switching Hobbies or Having Many

It is common for ADHD individuals to hop from one interest to another. This can feel like a flaw, but it is also a chance to explore variety. Here are ways to handle it healthily:

- **Keep a "Hobby Ideas" List**: Whenever you get a new idea, write it down. If you still like it after a few weeks, you can try it.
- **Set a Limit**: Maybe allow yourself two or three active hobbies at a time to avoid overwhelming yourself or your budget.
- **Return to Old Hobbies**: It is okay to circle back to something you did in the past. Hobbies can come and go in phases.

As long as you do not overspend or neglect responsibilities, exploring multiple hobbies can be a normal and enjoyable part of ADHD life.

18. Overcoming Guilt for "Unproductive" Fun

Some adults feel guilty spending time on hobbies if they are not obviously productive, especially if ADHD makes them behind on chores or work. But relaxation is important for mental health:

- **See Hobbies as Self-Care**: They recharge your energy, reduce stress, and can improve focus when you return to responsibilities.
- **Schedule Them**: By placing hobby time on your calendar, you treat it as valid as any other appointment.
- **Delegate or Simplify**: If chores pile up, look for small ways to lighten the load. A clean environment and handled responsibilities often free up mental space for guilt-free hobby enjoyment.

Balancing tasks with leisure is a healthy approach. You do not have to "earn" your right to have fun, but you also want to avoid letting your life spin out of control.

---

19. Recognizing the Role of Hobbies in Overall Well-Being

Pursuing activities you genuinely enjoy can support your mental health, relationships, and sense of identity. Hobbies can:

- **Boost Mood**: Creating or accomplishing something small can release positive feelings.
- **Reduce ADHD Frustrations**: Having an area where you feel free and not judged can offset daily struggles.
- **Foster Life Balance**: Work and family duties can be stressful. A hobby offers a break, enhancing overall emotional balance.
- **Enhance Skills**: You might discover talents that spill over into other areas of life, like better hand-eye coordination, problem-solving, or confidence in tackling new tasks.

When hobbies become part of your self-care, they can help round out your identity beyond the demands of daily life.

Chapter 19: When to Seek Professional Help

Living with ADHD can bring unique strengths: creativity, resourcefulness, and big-picture thinking, among others. Yet it also has real challenges that sometimes cannot be managed by willpower alone. There are times when self-guided efforts—like organization tools, mindfulness sessions, or family support—may not provide enough relief. In these moments, speaking with a professional can be essential. A psychologist, psychiatrist, therapist, or coach can lend expertise, strategies, and sometimes medication adjustments that create more stable daily routines and improve emotional balance.

This chapter looks at the signs that professional help might be wise. It also explains what kinds of support are available, how to prepare for a visit, and what it looks like to work with a trained expert. Seeking professional assistance is not an admission of failure; rather, it is a practical step toward greater stability and relief. By recognizing the right moment to talk with someone who specializes in ADHD or mental health, you can protect your well-being and maintain a healthier, happier life.

---

1. Signs That You Might Need Extra Support

1.1 Chronic Overwhelm While mild stress is normal, ongoing or intense overwhelm that does not improve, even when you try self-help strategies, can be a red flag. If day-to-day tasks—like making meals, going to work, or caring for children—feel nearly impossible, it is probably time to talk to a professional.

1.2 Extreme Emotional Swings Many women with ADHD have strong emotions, but if you feel trapped in cycles of anger, sadness, or anxiety and cannot break free, outside help may be essential.

Emotional swings can harm your relationships and daily functioning if left unaddressed.

1.3 Constant Failures in Organization Forgetting appointments, losing important items, or missing bill payments every now and then is one thing. However, if disorganization is causing large financial or social consequences, it might be beyond quick fixes. A trained expert can help you set up systems or adjust medication if needed.

1.4 Worsening Anxiety or Depression Some women with ADHD also have anxiety or depression, which can get worse over time. If you notice signs like ongoing worry, panic attacks, long-term sadness, or hopelessness, do not ignore them. Those symptoms may respond to therapy, medication, or both.

1.5 Relationship Troubles If fights or misunderstandings with your partner, friends, or family keep escalating, ADHD symptoms might play a part. You may lash out without meaning to, or struggle to communicate. Couples or family therapy guided by an ADHD-informed counselor can ease tensions.

1.6 Substance Use or Other Harmful Coping Some people with ADHD turn to alcohol, drugs, or unhealthy behaviors to handle stress. If this is happening frequently or escalating, it is a strong signal to seek professional aid. Substance use is not a solution for ADHD—it often causes bigger problems.

Any of these signs alone does not mean you have failed. Instead, view them as signals that you may need more tools or fresh perspectives. Outside specialists deal with similar issues every day and can guide you in practical, personalized ways.

2. Types of Professionals Who Can Help

Understanding your options can make the process of seeking help less confusing:

1. **Primary Care Doctor**: This might be your family doctor or a general physician. They can perform a basic evaluation, rule out other conditions (like thyroid issues), and sometimes prescribe ADHD medication. They might also refer you to specialists for further assessment.
2. **Psychiatrist**: A medical doctor specializing in mental health, including ADHD. Psychiatrists can diagnose, manage medications, and sometimes provide therapy.
3. **Psychologist or Therapist**: Trained in diagnosing and treating mental health issues through talk therapy, counseling, and behavioral techniques. They cannot prescribe medication (unless they also have a medical degree, which is rare), but they can collaborate with a psychiatrist if medication is needed.
4. **ADHD Coach**: Focuses on practical life strategies—time management, organization, goal-setting. Coaches are not typically licensed mental health professionals, so they do not diagnose or treat mental illness. But they can be a valuable resource for day-to-day coping methods.
5. **Counselors or Social Workers**: They might offer therapy or guidance on coping skills, relationships, or emotional support. Some have specialized ADHD training.

Choosing the right professional may depend on factors like your budget, insurance coverage, location, and whether you suspect other mental health conditions besides ADHD. For instance, if anxiety or depression is severe, you might see a psychologist or psychiatrist first. If you mainly need help with routines and structure, an ADHD coach could be a good fit.

3. Deciding Where to Start

3.1 Assess Your Primary Needs

- If disorganization is your main issue and you can manage emotionally, an ADHD coach might be enough.
- If you have deep sadness, panic, or strong mood swings, therapy or a psychiatrist might be more suitable.

3.2 Talk to Your Doctor Your general practitioner can give referrals to ADHD specialists or mental health professionals in your area. They may also do an initial screening or run blood tests to ensure there are no physical conditions mimicking ADHD symptoms.

3.3 Check Insurance or Financial Resources Some professionals might be covered by insurance, others not. If cost is a concern, ask about sliding-scale fees or public clinics.

3.4 Recommendations from Friends or Support Groups Personal referrals can help. If you know someone with ADHD who found a supportive doctor or counselor, that can be a great place to begin.

The point is to act when you feel daily life is becoming too much. Early intervention can prevent larger problems down the line.

---

4. The Evaluation Process

Seeing a professional for ADHD or mental health concerns typically involves:

1. **Initial Interview**: You share your background, current issues, health history, and any previous diagnoses or treatments. Being honest helps them form an accurate picture.

2. **Symptom Checklists**: They may ask you to fill out questionnaires about attention, organization, mood, or emotional patterns.
3. **Medical Screening**: Blood work or other tests can rule out conditions that might resemble ADHD, such as vitamin deficiencies or hormone imbalances.
4. **Discussion of History**: They might want to know if you had trouble focusing in childhood, as ADHD often starts early. If you were not diagnosed as a child, you can still have ADHD, but they need a full picture.
5. **Other Factors**: They will look for co-occurring issues like anxiety, depression, or learning disorders, since ADHD often does not exist alone.

After gathering information, the professional will talk about whether ADHD is the main issue or if other conditions are in play. They may recommend medication, therapy, coaching, or a combination.

---

5. Treatment Options

Professional help can take different forms:

5.1 Medication

- Stimulants (like methylphenidate or amphetamine-based meds) are commonly prescribed for ADHD. They can improve focus and reduce impulsivity in many individuals.
- Non-stimulant meds (like atomoxetine) might be used if stimulants are not well tolerated or if there are other considerations.
- Anti-anxiety or antidepressant medication could be considered if anxiety or depression is part of the picture.

5.2 Therapy

- **Cognitive Behavioral Therapy (CBT)**: Helps identify unhelpful thinking patterns and behaviors, teaching new coping methods for ADHD struggles.
- **Dialectical Behavior Therapy (DBT)**: Focuses on emotion regulation and mindfulness, which can be useful if strong emotions disrupt daily life.
- **Psychodynamic or Talk Therapy**: May help you understand your feelings and history more deeply, though it might not be as directly action-oriented for ADHD tasks.

5.3 Skills Coaching

- An ADHD coach or therapist might show you how to break tasks into smaller steps, create effective routines, and keep a balanced schedule. They might also guide you in planning, time estimation, and setting realistic goals.

5.4 Group Sessions

- Some clinics or community centers run ADHD support groups. Talking with others facing similar issues can provide moral support and fresh ideas.

5.5 Combined Approaches Often, medication plus therapy (and possibly coaching) yields the best results. Each piece addresses different aspects of ADHD. Medication can stabilize focus while therapy helps you build practical or emotional skills.

---

6. Overcoming Barriers to Seeking Help

6.1 Stigma and Shame You might worry that seeking therapy or ADHD medication signals weakness. Actually, it is a proactive step.

Everyone needs help sometimes, and mental health is as valid as physical health.

6.2 Time and Effort Finding a good provider might require research, phone calls, or waiting for appointments. If that feels daunting, ask a friend or family member for help or break the process into smaller tasks.

6.3 Cost Therapy or meds can be expensive. Explore options like community health clinics, telehealth services that offer lower fees, or group therapy. Some providers have sliding scales based on income.

6.4 Past Negative Experiences If you have tried therapy or meds before and it did not help, you might feel discouraged. But every provider is different, and your needs may have changed. The right match could make all the difference now.

6.5 Fear of Diagnosis Some people worry about labeling themselves. But a diagnosis can be a relief if it explains years of struggle. It also opens the door to targeted solutions rather than trial-and-error guessing.

---

7. How to Prepare for an Appointment

Before you see a mental health professional or doctor, a bit of prep can streamline the visit:

1. **Make a Symptom List**: Write down your main problems (forgetfulness, missing deadlines, extreme emotions, etc.), including when they started and how they affect your life.
2. **Note Past Treatments**: Recall if you have tried any ADHD medications, therapy, or organizational methods before. Mention what worked or did not.

3. **Identify Goals**: Think about what you want from treatment. Better focus at work? Less stress at home? Improved emotional balance?
4. **Gather Key History**: If possible, get records from childhood if you suspect long-standing ADHD. If that is not possible, no worries—you can still explain your experiences.
5. **Write Questions**: Examples: "What are the side effects of stimulant medication?" or "Do you offer therapy for emotional swings?" or "How often would we meet?"

A little organization beforehand helps you get the most out of the appointment, especially when ADHD can cause nervousness or memory lapses.

---

8. What to Expect in Therapy Sessions

If you start therapy, here is a rough outline of what might happen:

1. **First Session**: You and the therapist talk about your background, concerns, and therapy goals. This is also a time to see if you feel comfortable with their style.
2. **Ongoing Sessions**: You meet weekly or every other week. The therapist might introduce tasks or exercises, ask about how your week went, and help you apply coping methods to real-life problems.
3. **Homework**: CBT or other structured therapies often involve trying out new habits or journaling between visits.
4. **Progress Check**: Therapists will occasionally review how things are going. If something is not helping, they adjust the approach.
5. **Safe Space**: Therapy is confidential. You can discuss fears or mistakes without judgment. It is a zone to explore deeper feelings or hidden thoughts.

Therapy is not about someone telling you what to do, but guiding you to find and practice solutions that match your unique mind.

---

9. Medication Management

If medication is part of your plan:

- **Starting Slowly**: Doctors often begin with a low dose and see how you respond. They might adjust it every few weeks until they find a dose that balances benefits with minimal side effects.
- **Tracking Effects**: Writing down how you feel each day—energy levels, focus, mood—helps the doctor see if adjustments are needed.
- **Communicating Side Effects**: Common issues might be sleep trouble, appetite changes, or irritability. Always report them so the doctor can decide if a different dose or different medication is better.
- **Regular Check-Ins**: You might visit monthly or quarterly to confirm the medication still suits your changing life. If you notice a return of strong ADHD symptoms, you can discuss this and adjust as needed.

Medication alone does not cure ADHD, but it can give your brain the support needed to learn new habits or engage more fully in therapy.

---

10. Involving Loved Ones

If you have a partner, friend, or family member who is supportive, including them in the therapy or coaching process can help:

- **They Can Give Insight**: Sometimes, loved ones notice patterns that you do not see, like how your mood changes in the evening or how you react to stress.
- **Family or Couples Therapy**: If ADHD causes conflicts at home, therapy sessions with your spouse or other family members might address communication or responsibilities.
- **Encouragement**: Loved ones can help you remember appointments, track improvements, or practice new coping skills.

Still, it is your choice how much you share. If you want private one-on-one therapy, that is valid. But letting trusted friends or relatives know you are seeking help can bring extra understanding and kindness.

---

11. Life Changes During Treatment

With the right support, many women with ADHD see tangible shifts:

1. **Improved Daily Routines**: Over time, you might learn to create schedules, set reminders, and keep on top of tasks more reliably.
2. **Less Emotional Turmoil**: Therapy or medication can temper intense mood swings, giving you more control in heated moments.
3. **Higher Self-Esteem**: Feeling more capable often reduces self-blame. Achieving small successes—like managing finances or meeting deadlines—builds confidence.
4. **Better Relationships**: As you adopt healthier communication and coping, conflicts may become less frequent. You may also show more empathy for others' perspectives.

Progress might come in small steps. You might see immediate relief in one area (like better focus) but need more time for deeper emotional or habit changes. Treatment is a process, not a quick fix.

---

12. Knowing When to Switch Strategies

Sometimes a therapy method or medication that helped early on may lose effectiveness, or new life changes can create new challenges. If you feel stuck:

- **Share Concerns**: Tell your professional what is not working. They might suggest a new approach or combine methods.
- **Second Opinions**: It is okay to see another therapist or doctor if you feel your current one does not understand your needs.
- **Stay Open to Adjustments**: ADHD evolves over a lifetime. College stress differs from parenting demands. If your life shifts, your treatment might too.

The goal is to remain flexible so that your support system adapts to real-life changes rather than expecting you to force old solutions in new situations.

---

13. Addressing Co-Existing Conditions

Besides ADHD, many women face conditions like anxiety, depression, learning disorders, or postpartum challenges. Professional help is especially crucial if:

- **Anxiety**: You struggle with panic, obsessive worries, or social fears that limit daily life.

- **Depression**: You have low energy, negative thoughts, or feelings of worthlessness lasting for weeks or months.
- **Trauma**: Past experiences may still affect your thoughts, behaviors, or relationships.
- **Eating Disorders**: Binge eating, restrictive eating, or other patterns can be linked to emotional regulation difficulties.

Working with a specialist who recognizes co-occurring issues ensures you receive a thorough plan, not just a one-dimensional approach focusing solely on ADHD.

---

14. Handling Doubts About Medications

Medication worries are common. Some fear side effects, addiction potential, or personality changes. Here is how to address these concerns:

1. **Educate Yourself**: Read credible sources, speak to your doctor, and learn about medication facts vs. myths.
2. **Start Slow**: Many professionals begin at the lowest effective dose, reducing severe side effects or abrupt changes.
3. **Monitor**: Track how you feel physically and emotionally. If you notice problems, bring them up immediately. Medication is adjustable, and you have the right to switch or stop if needed.
4. **Lifestyle Factors**: Medication works best paired with healthy sleep, exercise, and a reasonable diet. Over-reliance on pills alone might not solve everything.

A balanced perspective acknowledges medication can be a tool—not a cure-all—and that constant communication with a doctor is key.

15. When Hospitalization or Intensive Care Is Necessary

Most ADHD treatments happen in outpatient settings, such as appointments every week or month. However, in rare situations:

- **Severe Suicidal Thoughts**: If you feel unsafe with your thoughts, a short hospital stay might be needed to protect you until the crisis subsides.
- **Extreme Depression or Manic Episodes**: If your emotions become dangerously unstable or you cannot function at all, an inpatient or partial hospitalization program might offer close monitoring.
- **Substance Rehabilitation**: If addiction complicates ADHD, inpatient detox or rehab might be recommended for a while.

These measures can feel scary, but they are temporary safety nets. With the right care, you can stabilize and return to your usual life with stronger coping resources.

---

16. Support Systems Beyond Professionals

While therapy and medication are vital, do not overlook other help:

- **Peer Support**: Online forums or local ADHD groups let you talk with people who truly understand. Exchanging tips or simply venting can be comforting.
- **Mentors**: A kind boss, teacher, or older friend might share life experience and guidance beyond formal therapy.
- **Family Agreements**: For example, if you tend to forget deadlines, a spouse or sibling can remind you gently or help you keep track if they know your signals.

Combining professional and personal support is often the best way to stay consistent and feel encouraged.

17. Maintaining Progress After Therapy

If you reach a point where therapy feels less necessary—maybe you have built better routines or your mood is stable—you might reduce sessions or stop entirely. However, ADHD is ongoing. You may want to:

1. **Stay in Touch**: Occasional "check-in" appointments keep you from falling back into old patterns.
2. **Self-Monitor**: Keep using the tools you learned—journaling, checklists, mindfulness—to catch early warning signs of overwhelm.
3. **Stay Flexible**: If life changes, you might revisit therapy or meet with a coach again. Seeking help in the future is not a failure; it is normal for ADHD to need renewed focus at different life stages.

---

18. Benefits of Long-Term Support

Some individuals choose ongoing therapy, coaching, or medication oversight. This can offer:

- **Stable Accountability**: Knowing you will talk to someone next week or next month can keep you motivated to practice new habits.
- **Deeper Self-Awareness**: Long-term therapy or coaching can reveal deeper patterns or emotional triggers you did not see at first.
- **Preventive Measures**: Regular check-ins may stop small concerns from growing into big crises.

If you can afford it and find it beneficial, there is no shame in a long-term relationship with a mental health professional or coach who truly understands ADHD.

Concluding Thoughts on a Bright Future

This book has offered insights on ADHD in women, covering everything from recognizing symptoms to building supportive routines. Although ADHD presents lifelong challenges, there is also room for satisfaction, success, and joy. You can focus effectively, maintain fulfilling relationships, and manage daily tasks with less stress by blending practical strategies with compassion for yourself.

Your future remains open-ended, shaped by how you choose to handle ADHD's tests and harness its gifts. Even if you face difficult days or new stumbling blocks, you now have knowledge, tools, and hopefully a supportive network. As you continue learning and adjusting, you can transform struggles into growth.

Be patient with yourself: progress can be slow, but each step forward—whether it is refining a habit or pausing before a hasty decision—builds a steadier life. Remember to acknowledge small wins, to ask for help when needed, and to keep exploring fresh methods if old ones stop working. In the end, ADHD may remain part of your story, but it does not have to write the entire script. Your choices, perseverance, and sense of hope shape who you become, giving you the ability to live with ADHD in a calmer, more empowered way.

Over these chapters, we discussed how ADHD impacts women in areas like school, work, organization, stress, relationships, and beyond. We touched on practical approaches—time management, therapy, medication, mindfulness, and others—that can ease daily strain. While ADHD is an ongoing condition, it is possible to find routines and supports that reduce the burdens and highlight your strengths.

www.ingramcontent.com/pod-product-compliance
Lightning Source LLC
LaVergne TN
LVHW012042070526
838202LV00056B/5560